abraca
DAMMIT!
DISASTER STORIES & LIFE LESSONS
FROM THE WORLD'S TOP MAGICIANS

DEDICATED TO

MR. BILL & HELEN ANDREWS

BILL HERZ

MOM & DAD

RITA BARNHART

ALIXY ZABIN

THE STAGGS

DAVID ROSENSTEIN

PHOEBE BROOK

DEREK MCKEE

DARREN ROMEO

TABLE OF CONTENTS

INTRODUCTION

This is likely the only magic book you will read that came about as a result of a mistake. Three days prior to the moment I write this, I had the biggest blunder of my entire life (which so far has been eighteen years, eight months, and twenty-five days). It all happened at the Rio Hotel and Casino in Las Vegas in front of Penn and Teller... plus a thousand people in the live audience. CWTV was shooting "Penn and Teller: Fool Us," and I was lucky enough to be a contestant. The act I chose to perform required me to borrow the phone of the hostess- Alyson Hannigan. Part of the method's trickery involved hiding her phone in a secret location unbeknownst to the audience. During this performance, however, her phone slipped out of its secret location and hit the floor with a dramatically loud thud.

Now I know what you might be thinking, but let me assure you that I had practiced and performed this routine hundreds of times. Neither my multiple outs, backup plans, nor scripted ad libs could have prepared me for this moment. Even though this blunder had never happened before, luck would ensure that disaster struck during this biggest performance of my life.

Although my act ended up being cut from the season I now have an incredible tale to tell as well as a valuable lesson learned. Furthermore this experience provided me with a new thought process and approach to magic "horror stories".

Every magician has had mistakes happen to them, but the best magicians utilize these tragedies to learn and to grow as professionals. With this in mind, I compiled this anthology of the errors (and subsequent lessons learned) that helped shape some of our industry's greatest performers into who they are today.

The magicians included in this publication have provided their time, ideas, honesty, and knowledge. I couldn't have done my part without their generosity and have trouble expressing my gratitude into words. The contributors and I hope that you will learn from their mistakes. Embrace these performers' flops by educating yourself so that it won't happen to you. Read, learn, then go out, perform, and make some mistakes of your own!

The quest for perfection hinders us from becoming stronger magicians, performers, and people.

How to read this book:

While composing this book, I wanted to create more than a basic compilation of essays. I wanted this to be a cherished collection of candid conversations. Imagine if someone transcribed TEDTalks delivered by exceptional professionals in our field. When interviewing each contributor over the phone or Skype, I asked each performer the same series of open-ended questions. They were given the option to take their answers in whatever direction they chose to encourage truly genuine responses. The questions asked were:

- *What was the biggest mistake you ever made in your professional career?*
- *What was the best life lesson you were ever taught?*
- *What is one piece of advice you would give another entertainer?*
- *What/who has been a crucial resource to you and your career?*
- *What has been an "oh shit!" moment for you?*

The answers drastically differed depending on the magician. I wrote down the answers verbatim to each question during the interview and afterwards I composed a second draft with minimal edits that ensured cohesiveness, without jeopardizing the message.

I would like to thank each magician for their contribution to this book. These professionals maintain jam-packed calendars, and I am so incredibly grateful to each one for taking time out of their busy schedules to speak with me. All of them volunteered to be a part of this project and are making exactly $0 from this book. However, many of these contributors have created and sell books, lecture notes, tricks, and videos. As much as this small book can provide, you can further learn invaluable information from these other resources, and it is my hope that you will support the magicians in our community by investing in their products. I promise you won't be disappointed. *-Ben Zabin, 2017*

Scott Alexander is known in the magic world for his high impact stand up magic. His funny and likeable charm makes him a favorite among all audiences. He was a finalist on America's Got Talent, a guest on the Oprah Winfrey Show, headlined at Caesar's Palace in Las Vegas for seven years, and directed and starred in "Elements"- a million dollar show produced by Norwegian Cruise Lines. A few weeks after I interviewed him, I was fortunate enough to see him lecture in Long Island. Watching him work for an overcrowded room of magicians showed me firsthand why this man is in such high demand among the magic club and convention circuit. I left with newfound knowledge and inspiration while having had a fabulous time watching a true master work.

"Be so good they can't ignore you."

Steve Martin said that and I think it's the best piece of advice I was ever taught. If you're going to pursue a career in magic, you have to be good. The only way to be good is to practice! If you just go to a magic shop, buy a trick, and just start doing it, it's going to suck. And if it somehow manages to not be terrible, then it certainly won't be as good as it could have been had you practiced it. When practicing, be sure to rehearse in costume. My wife and I were driving to a show in Texas and on the way we stopped at a store where my wife saw a hair extension wig that clipped onto the back of her bun to make it look better. Anyways, it looked nice so she bought it and wore it in the show that night! The show was going well, and one of our routines was a sub trunk. I get in the box, she ties me up in the bag, hops on top of the box, throws up the sheet, and I'm all of a sudden on top in my triumphant pose! The audience applauds and then I hear them laughing. I look down and the wig had gotten caught on the button of my jacket. It's hanging so low that it looks like a ton of pubic hair sticking out... that or a furry critter! I yank it off, and in the heat of the moment start doing Rocky Raccoon moves up my arm, and then I throw it off the stage. Had we practiced it in our full costumes that wouldn't have happened and from then on we started practicing the right way, because that will help ensure that what you have planned is what's going to happen. But then again sometimes, it just doesn't always work out that way.

I was doing a show in Mesquite, Nevada (about an hour north of Las Vegas) at the CasaBlanca Resort and Casino. The client had asked for a big show, so I decided to rent a tiger. (By the way, it's a really shitty idea to rent a tiger.) Anyway, a few days before the gig I get a call from the animal trainer who tells me he is double booked and needs to take another one of his animals to a movie shoot. He reassured me that he can send his assistant, and although it wasn't ideal, I agreed. The day of the show the assistant trainer shows up with the tiger, we rehearse, and everything goes great- the tiger does what it's supposed to do, does the pose, and it all works out fine. At around 3:00pm, after the rehearsal for the show that night, the assistant trainer puts the tiger back in the cage and leaves. However the door to the cage hadn't closed properly and the next thing I know the tiger had walked out of the cage, through an open door leading outside, and right into the parking lot. In broad daylight, in the middle of the desert, there's a tiger walking around through the cars, just looking around! Someone called 911 and within five minutes, police had surrounded the area, helicopters were in the air, and shotguns were set up ready to shoot the tiger, who at this point was just lying on the ground playing with some wire he had found. Before they were about to shoot the tiger, I jump in front with a big slab of chicken and start making a sound that I was told supposedly comforts tigers. He sees me and the chicken, and I slowly start leading it back to the cage. I throw the chicken in, the tiger follows, the assistant trainer comes to close the cage (properly this time), and the onlookers leave. I thought for sure the show would be cancelled, but the client told me that this incident got so much press coverage and attention that the show was now sold out!

Unless you're a tiger who has gotten loose, never eat less than two hours before a show. I was doing my residency at Caesars Palace in Las Vegas and was on my way to the show. I stopped off at a restaurant* and ate some meat about 45 minutes before the show. I was about to go onstage and as I'm lighting torches backstage (we opened with a fire cage) I realize I wasn't feeling well. The stage hand decides to give me a bottle of Perrier and BAM- I throw up everywhere. It turns out I came down with a rapid dose of food poisoning! The show starts, we do the opener, and then as my wife goes into her linking ring routine, I go backstage and throw up again. This happens again and again until basically between every trick I was offstage throwing up. We close with the sub trunk and the stage hand puts a bucket in the box. The second I'm in the box, my head goes straight to the bucket and I throw up for the last time. We finish the show, and it's not until a long time after that that I returned to that restaurant.

Years later I learned yet another lesson. I have something that I call my Oprah moment. I get a call one morning from a representative of Oprah and they want me to come out and be on a segment they're doing about people who are living their childhood dreams.

*Due to legal reasons, we can't say what this restaurant is.
But they serve Tacos, and they ring a Bell.

I asked if they wanted me to do any magic, and they said there probably wouldn't be time, because all she wanted was an interview. Just to be safe, I bring a cigarette paper tear. The shoot starts and I'm sitting in the front row of the audience and she comes up to me, asks my name, and what I do. In my mind, I'm debating if I should show her the trick or not, and I ultimately decide to hold off until I find a better moment. However, as soon as I answer the first question, some other lady interrupts and starts going on and on about something not that interesting. When I'm about to interject to segue into my trick, Oprah wraps up the show, saying they were out of time.

Right then and there I realized I should have taken the opportunity the moment when I had it, which is when she first addressed me. Had I done so, I would have gotten more air time and it would have been very beneficial to me. What I learned from this is if you have a chance to jump at something- anything- TAKE IT. If you have an opportunity, don't hesitate. TAKE IT. Before I moved to Las Vegas, I was working for a magician in Florida. I got a call for a one-night corporate gig in Las Vegas and asked the magician if I could take a couple nights off to go do the show. He said yes, and I flew off to Vegas. When I got there I walked up and down the strip and fell in love with it. I didn't want to go to sleep! This was a heaven to me. I came across Caesar's Magical Empire, walked/snuck in ,and immediately knew that this is where I wanted to be. I asked someone how I could get to perform here, and he gave me the information of the booker. The booker got back to me immediately and asked me to come audition tomorrow. I was supposed to fly back to Florida then. However, this was something I really wanted to do, so I called up the magician's wife who said if I wasn't back by tomorrow night then I wouldn't have a job anymore. However, I decided to TAKE that opportunity. The booker liked me and told me to keep in touch but didn't have anything available, so I flew back home without a job waiting for me. I called back a week later to follow up and turns out that a spot had just opened up! I was to fly back out to fill in for an act (The Pendragons) for a few weeks. Those few weeks ended up turning into seven years, all because I took the opportunity that was available.

Ed Alonzo is easily recognized as one of the country's foremost comedy magicians. Starting off in The Magic Castle's junior program, he went on to win the coveted "Stage Magician of the Year" award for two years in a row, and then "Comedy Magician of the Year" for another two years in a row, and then finally the renowned "Magician of the Year" in 2010. He's had multiyear headline contracts in Las Vegas, carried out command performances for royalty in London, and has countless US and international television appearances under his belt. You may recognize him from his appearances on The Ellen Degeneres Show, Top Chef, Cupcake Wars, The Late Show with Craig Ferguson, America's Next Top Model, How I Met Your Mother, Modern Family, Masters of Illusion, E-True Hollywood Story, and many, many more. He's toured and performed with Britney Spears and has created illusions for Michael Jackson, Katy Perry, and David Blaine.

Early on in my career I was the polar opposite onstage as to what I am now. I was trying to be something I wasn't- the suave and futuristic magician. I was in the junior program at the Magic Castle with Mark Kalin, and he was the flashy magician- I wanted to be like him. This led to the biggest mistake I made, which was not realizing I needed to find a character that was me onstage in order to make it all work. This mistake came from not looking at myself with open eyes, which resulted in what I'm sure were many lost opportunities. Instead of looking at myself, I was looking at other magicians and wanting to be like them instead of being myself. It wasn't until I was at an acting audition that the director had me put on glasses and read the part again that I realized that there was something in this bud of a character that really fit me. I tried this newfound character out in a show and it kind of worked! Initially, I was just a nerdy guy with a squeaky voice. But I learned this wasn't enough. I wanted my audience to think that this character is how I was all the time, which would make me more likeable and more loveable. But how would I make this character believable? I wanted people to expect that I am no different offstage than onstage.

I learned that in order to make a strong character, you have to know that character inside and out, and know exactly what your character would do in any situation. This strong sense of your character comes by one thing, and one thing only- doing as many shows as you can. You have to find out what works for your audience, and what works for you, and this only comes from performing as often as possible. In addition to acting, I have always been a student of improvisation, and I still to this day take classes at The Groundlings. Improv studios teach that you have to free your mind, because when having nothing prepared, you go on an adventure of listening to characters and the audience, and working with that. As magicians, we do just that, but with props in our hands.

I've always said that the greatest trick I do is fooling the audience into thinking I'm someone I'm not. When people leave my magic show, I love that in the lobby you can hear them talking, and I like to be remembered as the guy with the spiky hair and glasses. If I wanted, I could walk out into the lobby after the show with a t-shirt and jeans and nobody would recognize me as the guy that was just onstage doing a show. Even walking into a dealers room at a convention, most people (except for some close friends) won't recognize me. I like that!

Another point that I wish I had figured out sooner is knowing my environment and situation. I was performing in this big production show in Las Vegas with dancers and variety acts and everything. One of the tricks I did was where I produced a girl out of a big fish tank who was dressed as a mermaid and would then proceed to do a water levitation. (It was cool- she had this big tail that would flap around.) Anyways, I carry her out of the fish tank where she appeared in and up the stairs to the platform where the water levitation was. I lay her on the platform, the water pushed her up, she began to float, and it was a beautiful effect. She came down, and there was a blackout. In the blackout, I had to rush down the stairs of the platform back to the stage and walk forward to take my big bow. But in the dark as I'm coming down the staircase I slip and my hands shot out to break the fall. I landed, and then proceeded to slide across the 6 inch plexiglass rim of the prop trying to keep the water from splashing out. I look down and my hand was cut almost in half, with blood gushing out. A stagehand threw me a towel to hold onto as I was taking my bow, which ended up turning into the color changing cloth trick! But I still had another 10 minutes of performance- the strait jacket and duck act. It was a bloody mess (with my strait jacket also changing color) but I managed to get through it. That experience taught me two things... that I needed to make my tricks baby proof and that I really had no business doing illusions that large. I realized that I was getting more reactions doing smaller tricks than a big giant trick. Looking back at the greats- like Billy McComb- I realized they were all the biggest personalities in the room and didn't need the tricks to speak for them.

When you're a magician full time, there is no spare time. There is no greater hobby for me than that of my career- I wouldn't know what could be more fun than creating, designing, and performing magic for people! I'm blessed to do what I like to do and so fortunate that it is what I do for my livelihood.

If you've ever seen a magician tear a newspaper into pieces and then restore it, chances are you were watching the genius of **Gene Anderson**. Some of the interviews in this book took 15 minutes... others took close to 40. However, for well over an hour, Gene allowed me to pick his brain and he went above and beyond the questions I asked! It was incredibly difficult to whittle down all the incredible material he offered. He had so many invaluable stories, tips, and ideas, and I wish I could have included all of them. However, he recently released an absolutely phenomenal book, "Gene Anderson: The Book", and I highly suggest you get yourself a copy. Between the covers is a wealth of information that every magician will find invaluable.

I grew up in northern Minnesota and there were no magic clubs or conventions so I never joined the magic community until I was in graduate school. It didn't mean I didn't do some magic, but it meant that there was no social organized magic where I was living. In graduate school I became the president of the magic club at the University of Texas in Austin where I was studying for my PhD as a chemist. I was organizing our Christmas show and inviting all kinds of guests like the people in my lab and their wives and whoever else. My graduate advisor, unbeknownst to me, was already planning a party. His party conflicted with my magic show, and he invited all the same people that had already committed to mine. So my guests told the boss that they couldn't go to his party because they were going to my magic show! That pissed him off, I guess, because he said "thanks to Gene, we can't have the party." I said I was "sorry that my planned event of two months ago conflicts with your plan as of yesterday" which probably wasn't a smart thing to say! What I learned from that, which was a life lesson, was that because he was the God of his empire, and here was a tiny little portion of it that which he wasn't but I was, he couldn't handle that. This taught me to not conflict my magic with whatever else my career may be.

So when I went to Dow Chemical, which is where I had my career. For the first 3 years, I didn't do any magic there... I laid low. They knew I was a magician, but they never saw me perform. However, one day a boss said he needed a magician for a Christmas party, and asked me to do it. I quoted him my regular asking price. He replied "hey, you're well snuffed so your price isn't an issue at all!" So Dow became, and still is, my biggest client. But you would never ever come into my office and see me do any tricks. I had total separation of Church and State. If you're going to be a part time magician, be a professional in both fields.

Never stop working on your routines. Do what scientists do, the scientific method:

1. Define the experiment
2. Gather data
3. Interpret results
4. Record the conclusion

Define each routine in your show as an experiment. Every show you do is an experiment and if you're not gathering data on it, you're missing something. Look at each show like this and plan ahead of time to gather data. How will you gather data? One way is to record it. An audio recording is better than a video recording. It will remind you of what happened in the show. If you watch a video recording of your show, the visual will overwhelm your brain. However, if you're recalling what you did in the show, that's stronger. Once you've gotten these recollections, write up your observations. Identify, and then improve things. I still record every show I do and write each one up. *(To see an example of how Gene writes up his shows, check out the 'Part Time Pro' section of his book "Gene Anderson: The Book")*

My first mentor was Cleve Haublud. He was getting his PhD while I was getting mine and I told him I was interested in going to my first magic convention- the Texas Association of Magicians (TAOM) Convention. Cleve told me that if I just went to see it, nobody would know who I was. But if I went and and competed, people would know who I was. I had a fledgling newspaper act that I took there, and I won! This was the start of my signature newspaper act and a lot of great things happened as a result.

In order for something to become a signature piece it has to endure a million mistakes over the years. For the most part, things in my act aren't original. I start with somebody else's ideas and take them to a different place.

I didn't choose newspaper... newspaper chose me. I realized that I could play this to an audience, so when I started developing it I said to myself "OK, these are the things I have, but one by one I'm going to replace these things with something better." That was my philosophy for the newspaper act. In my head I thought I was going to replace the 'Cornstalk From Newspaper' since it's been around for hundreds of years. However, I learned that that's impossible to replace! I learned this by listening to the audience, and now it's part of the signature! Somebody else will decide if what you're doing is a signature piece or not. If it's what you're being booked to do, then it's a signature piece!

When he was 20, **Jon Armstrong** became Disney World's resident magician- an unheard of feat for a guy that age. He spent five years there until he joined Caesar's Magical Empire in Las Vegas, where in-between runs he would tour the world as a performer and a lecturer. He's appeared on *The Today Show, The Tonight Show, Penn and Teller: Fool Us, The Bachelorette, Magic Castle After Dar*k, and *Masters of Illusion*. He's been featured on the cover of Magic and Genii magazine, and in the pages of the New York Times, LA Magazine, and Harpers. He's consulted on films such as The *Mentalist, Spiderman 3*, and *Ant Man* and more recently, he starred in the Netflix documentary *Magicians: Life in the Impossible*.

When I was younger, I was a big fan of guys like Bill Malone and Al Goshman, so as a kid I would be way too sarcastic and aggressive- which was so weird coming from a teenager! I would say lines that Bill Malone would say like "oh, that girl wants me!" When I got my show at Disney in Florida, I was still trying to embrace this character. However, doing that Bill Malone line to a girl at Disney didn't result in laughs, but complaints. Within the first three weeks, I was having sit down meetings with my manager and having to apologize. It was really, really bad. Needless to say I was forced to learn fast, so that was probably one of the biggest mistakes I made in my early career.

But then there are mistakes that happen, where it's not entirely my fault, but the audience views it as that. There was this time when I was doing a bit where I would walk through the crowd and assign roles to people "oh this person is the mean person" and just generic improv bits. This was still in my Disney days, but a little bit older than I was when I was using Bill Malone's lines. One of those bits I would assign someone to the character of Roger and say to them "oh boy! Roger, wow- he wasn't a very smart man... he wasn't the brightest bulb on the tree" and I would put my hand on somebody's shoulder- basically saying this is the guy I'm talking about. But once I didn't realize that the shoulder I had put my hand on was the shoulder of someone who obviously had Down Syndrome. Now I've done this bit a trillion times and it's always gotten laughs, but in this scenario I put my hand on the person but it gets no laughs. I look down and I realize that I screwed up. I could essentially see my contact getting destroyed, and I couldn't see a reason for them to keep me on. But I somehow played it off, by looking at the person and saying "this guy knows Roger! He knows how bad he is", and I think I got away with it, nobody said anything, but it was tense. It was one of those things where I immediately realized that I have to be much more aware of my situation and have to reflect what I say and do.

Another mistake I made, again happened early on in my career. I was booked to do magic on a casino boat- where they go out three miles, gamble, and come back in. The waters were really choppy that day and the food I ate earlier didn't agree with me. So I'm onstage and the ocean is moving and I am feeling SUPER queasy. I end up just... pooping my pants there on stage while holding back vomit. I ruin my suit, I have to close the show, and of course I never got hired again by those people.

There's accidents, and there's direct mistakes. I made a constant mistake throughout my twenties (I'm 41 now and fortunately I learned from them) of genuinely not listening to my audience. Not listening to what they were saying, not being as responsive as I should have been, and not knowing where I was in those moments. But if listen, your audience can essentially write your show for you. That was a mistake because I was in my own zone doing my own thing and the audience be damned of what I was trying to accomplish.
Then offstage, I made mistakes by doing stupid things that involved clients! I realized very quickly that when dealing

with clients you shouldn't be doing anything aside from being the most professional you can possibly be at any gig and knowing that people are always watching you. So when you hit on that girl and that girl turns out to be the client's daughter, that's not a smart move. You have to be aware of what your role is as the professional magician.

Throughout my career I never learned anything by talking. I learned everything by shutting my mouth and listening to what someone else said. If I can give any piece of advice both as a performer and as a person, it would be to listen. You don't have to take everything you hear. I thought early on that everything you hear is right and applicable to you. It sometimes isn't, but I realized that no matter what it is, you should listen. Don't respond back by debating, just listen. If someone gives you advice, don't disagree with them. Don't get into an argument! Just accept it and walk away from it and process it. Debate it in your own head, because even if you don't agree with what they said, it could spark a new idea or thought. The moment that you defend your act, you're defending nothing. If you're constantly defending your act, you're defending something that's not worth defending. I learned everything I ever learned by NOT talking.

The best resource to my career is a man named Terry Ward. He is the only full time, resident magician at Walt Disney World. He's been performing there for 28 years, does five shows a day, five days a week, fifty weeks a year and has been having a blast all these years. Nobody has done more magic than him, and that's not counting all of the other gigs he does on top of that. He also does corporate gigs and trade show gigs both for Disney and other clients. Mathematically, nobody's done more magic! If you're doing five 30 minute shows a day, five days a week, fifty weeks a year, that's 625 hours of magic shows a year! So basically he's really skilled at his act.

What I learned from him is not to have the show feel robotic to the audience, how to give each audience a new approach, and to make them feel that what is about to happen has never happened before. He's really good at that! He's also really good at understanding people and knows all about the relationship between the performer and the audience and he's been my mentor! I saw him when I was fourteen and I told myself that this was what I wanted to do for the rest of my life and he became sort of like a father to me and is someone who I still to this day speak to at least weekly, and he's the guy who I run all my bits and material past. He won't tell me about my moves or sleights, but he'll say "this might work for this type of audience, but you might want to try that line here, that might not play, etc". Terry is the one who pre-audience tests something for me. He's going to be able to tell me where the strength or weaknesses are going to be and how it would play for most audiences, because he's performed for all audiences.

One time as I was entering a gig where I was going to do walk around, I was told a few people wouldn't speak English. I said "okay, I can handle that", but then I quickly realized that none of them spoke English. Not a single person in the room! I thought I would get around it by pointing and gesturing. Fine! But it turns out that not only were these people all French, but they were all very religious... Hassidic Jews. So all the rules about touching/talking to women applied, so not only did I have to deal with the language barrier, but I had to deal with the cultural and religious sensitivity at the same time. They didn't even want to look at cards because it was against their religion! I had no idea how the hell I was going to get out of this. Why did they want a magician? It was so weird. But I did it!

Thank God I had rubber bands and a set of sponge bunnies. All I did that night was was linking rubber bands and sponge bunnies because that was all they could watch! But none of this was told to me when the gig was booked... none of it. But they ended up sitting back and watching what I could do. That night I learned that pretty much everyone wants magic. There are people who you might think aren't the target audience for your show but who still want to see what you're offering. If you are able to connect just a little bit and show them something neat, they'll like it! This was the closest I've ever been to performing in that pure magic style. I've always performed in a comedic style (I'm a funny person who does magic). Here I could be a little funny, but it was really the magic that was being focused. We were making a major connection despite vast differences, and that was great! You can still connect with people that are different for you, providing what you are doing is miraculous.

There was another time when I was doing a walk around gig for a group that I was told consisted of people who were big partiers. I get in and the entire room is all little people. ALL dwarfs. There were a couple people of full height, but they were pretty much all dwarfs. It was weird! It was a total shock. I made it a point to sit down and gather the people around me so we were all at the same level, and I got a table and performed like I would at The Magic Castle! But once we were all situated, I began performing for them like I would for anybody, and it was great, it was fun! Everyone was having a good time. I think the initial shock of walking into the room was what was really strange to me. Because again, I was not told what this was going to be. I had no idea. And just being able to adapt to the space was a great lesson. I'm glad that those experiences happened to me in my thirties, as opposed to my twenties. In my early twenties, I don't know how I would have reacted and I don't know how good I would have been. I may not have come out of those situations looking like a professional, or somebody who was doing a good job. But fortunately I had learned a lot from my entire experience of doing magic and both those instances ended up being a success.

"You build on failure. You use it as a stepping stone. Close the door on the past. You don't try to forget the mistakes, but you don't dwell on it. You don't let it have any of your energy, or any of your time, or any of your space."

-Johnny Cash

I first met **Michael Carbonaro** in 2012 at Tannen's Magic Camp where he kindly helped me with an act I was preparing for a competition. Nobody knew then that in just a couple of years he would go from doing private parties to being a household name. During his live tour in 2017 I had the good fortune to join his team and help out with a dozen or so shows. Working with him on my act at Camp and then working with him on his tour showed me that he was the exact same nice, caring, gracious, funny, helpful, and selfless man both before and after he hit fame. If you haven't yet, be sure to check out his TV and Live show! I promise you'll become a huge fan in no time.

Let me start by saying that show business just doesn't make a whole lot of sense. There is no direct, sure fire path to success. Half of it is your talent, half is the choices you make, and the other halves are preparation and luck. I know, that's too many halves, but I told you, "It doesn't make a whole lot of sense."

Sometimes it's hard to know if you are doing something right versus "making a mistake." I think sometimes mistakes are more like the late painter Bob Ross put them – "happy accidents." They can lead to really good things! When a mistake happens on stage, maybe because of a little mess-up, the audience sometimes perks up and gets electrified! They can feel when something is a mistake or went the way it shouldn't have. And all the better if they watch it resolve. When I'm an audience member, I love getting that feeling! I love it when a show starts and maybe, say a microphone stand looks like it's falling and someone in the cast grabs it and saves it and the whole crowd kind of goes, "Whoa!" Call me crazy, but to me, that makes for a better show as it unifies us, the audience. Mistakes can also be precious. Part of the reason people like watching jugglers, for example, is because they may drop something at any time.

With magicians, it's a bit different. We often think we are making a mistake, but the audience really has no idea what we have planned so the mistake isn't always seen or as intense as we think or feel it is while performing. There is time to fix it, to cover it up, or make a joke out of. A mistake can even lead to a really funny line or perhaps... the greatest moment in our show. As much as we may panic when a mistake seems to rear its ugly head, it really can lead to good things – or at least really good memories!

With a live audience, it's a two-way street. You throw something out and it bounces back to you with a certain energy. You have that instant response (or not!) so you know (if) you're making a connection and can make decisions with that energy right now, right in the room. Performing for television is a different animal. For example, when I'm producing my hidden-camera, magic TV show, "The Carbonaro Effect," first I film all the content, then assemble it into a show, and THEN put it out there to the masses. Think of that – the audience response happens so much later. Months later. Nobody – including myself, anyone on the magic team, or crew – knows exactly how well we're doing as we're doing it. Even if, while shooting, we get great reactions and fool the pants off the people in the room, it is going to look and feel different through the camera, and assembled later into a complete half hour show in front of a viewing audience. It really isn't until we have a completely finalized product and air it on TV that we start getting feedback. So, if we need to make an adjustment on something, it's too late. We just have to learn from the home audience reaction to the episode and remember for "next time" …if there is one. The delayed timeline can be odd and confusing.

Now the good thing about TV is that if something happens that's an absolute disaster, well, we don't have to show it to anyone! With a live show… that's different! You can find yourself in a real jam with all eyes upon you. My most memorable instance of this experience was when I was a teenager and performing an illusion show on Long Island at an Easter event for a nun convent. (Yes, you read that right!) My assistant and I were performing Houdini's famous escape-switcheroo called "Metamorphosis." The magician gets locked inside a trunk, the assistant stands on top, and in an instant toss of a curtain, they have switched places! The magician is now standing on the trunk and the assistant is locked inside! My Dad and I made our version together at home and when we built the rod for the curtain top that goes around the box, we didn't use aluminum or plastic – we used steel, which was very heavy and really thick. Now, back at the nun convent, the ceilings were, let's say, lower than we had anticipated. So during the course of the trick, I got locked in the box, my assistant stood on top, she lifted up the curtain, and the metal bar smashed into the uncovered fluorescent light tubes that were hung from the ceiling! Yes sir! They all smashed in a loud shattering "POP!" There was a shower of glass and white powder that came down all over me and my assistant! At that moment, in our secret hidden vortex of the "Metamorphosis," we just said, "Keep going!" and I appeared on top of the box. (Now, I should say that if magicians were in the room, they might have noticed that the glass and white powder seemed to fall and "not fall" in different areas that don't match the laws of gravity quite right.) Anyway, I finished the trick, jumped down, unlocked the box, my assistant popped out, and we bowed and smiled. There was applause, and it seemed, also, like there was a huge elephant in the (now slightly less illuminated) room. At the end of the show, I didn't know what to say, I was so embarrassed. The nuns came over to us, and to my surprise, they were blown away by the trick! (Thank God we finished it!) They had nothing but huge appreciation and excitement about the show, saying how amazing it was, and how they were so sorry that "their lights fell on us!" I was stunned! Did they not see what we did?! What do I do? Oh my God, do I lie to the nuns? Yes. I quickly said "Oh hey it's no problem, it's okay. You know what? Everybody is okay and no one got hurt!" Man, I thought I was so slick. I didn't fess up, but I did offer to pay for the lights. (A bizarre inconsistency in my lying.) They were very grateful, but absolutely refused to take any money. It ended up being an adorable and sweet little moment and... they hired me back the next year! Looking back now, I do think they knew that my assistant and I smashed the lights, but at the time I really thought I got away with it. That was really cool of them. Er, I hope publishing this serves as a legit form of confession.

Granted, this didn't lead to any huge miracle, or great line, and it's certainly not something I started incorporating in to my show! But, the lesson here was strong..."Keep Going." Had we stopped the show because of the accident, not one single person in the room – myself and assistant included – would have been better for it. The show went on! And man oh man, put yourself in that audience's shoes. It all happened live and in real-time. For what it's worth (which is $83.94 - six florescent bulbs at $13.99 each), everyone in the room felt like they were part of a once in a lifetime experience – something that probably would never happen again. It's funny now for me to think there may just be a nun somewhere on Long Island, sitting in the dark, illuminated by only a TV, watching "The Carbonaro Effect" thinking, "Hey! That's the one who smashed our lights!"

Speaking of that there show, "The Carbonaro Effect," another mistake or "happy accident" that I can recall happened while shooting the pilot episode. Obviously with any TV show or movie, the final product that people see on the screen is just the tip of the iceberg of what goes on. We had one week in Georgia to put the whole pilot together. For one segment, we rented the whole floor of an office building but it was pretty empty as our pilot budget did not provide for a cast of realistic-looking background office workers to occupy the floor. The only "players" were the magic team at the time: David Regal, Johnny Thompson, John (Handsome Jack) Lovick, and myself. Jack was playing my "boss," and David and Johnny walked around the vast empty hallways, desperately trying to make this look like a functioning, busy office complex. (Good luck!)

Being a hidden-camera show, the spectators – who we call "Marks" – have no idea that anything magical is about to happen. In this case they were just unsuspecting people hired to do some office temp work. The trick was to convince the "Mark" of a teleportation device that could send objects from one side of the office to the other. For example, if someone needed a key down the hall, we could simply teleport it to them. There was a little machine that, in essence, was a secret magic prop that could seem to make the key vanish and return. Mixed with some sleight of hand, and "planned accidents," the effect was a real fooler.

Once we were all set to run the trick upstairs, the plan was to have Regal meet the "Marks" in the lobby and bring them up in the elevator to me. At one point, while we were resetting the trick between "Marks," our entire production team was standing around, talking about what could make the trick funnier or more magical when suddenly, a stranger walked into the room and began asking questions and... we slowly realize that it's the Mark! She had wandered upstairs by herself and somehow found our floor! We didn't want to lose the opportunity because we were on such a tight schedule and budget we didn't have the option to let her go. We just had to do it. So we all kind of silently nodded to each other and together just started talking our way around it, saying things like "Oh so nice to have you here! We're just finishing up a floor meeting," while we nonchalantly set up the trick, putting our backs in front of each part of the prop while others explained how the office worked. We ended up resetting the magic and got everyone into their secret places – their camera hides and wherever else they needed to be – and we pulled off the trick! It went amazingly smoothly, and that is the "Mark" that ended up airing on TV! She was completely fooled, even though she basically saw us resetting it while we, on a dime, improvised our way around being normal people in an office! In retrospect, I do believe that the mistake here helped to make the barren office environment seem like a real functioning space with all those people bustling about doing different things to get ready. The lesson, of course again… Keep Going! The audience does not know what you are about to do anyway… and you can get away with just about anything. Except smashing florescent lights with a steel pole.

My first encounter with **Jeff and Tessa Evason** was when my good friend and mentor Bill Herz brought his son, Zack, and I to a show they were doing at a college in the Bronx. We showed up about 45 minutes early and walked into a gorgeous 900 seat theater. They were all set and ready to go, and it looked as it was going to be the perfect show. A few minutes before the show Bill, Zack, and I went out in the lobby to wait before the doors opened and we saw a line of exactly three people. We thought the rest of the audience would show up late, but the rest of the audience turned out to be a mere 30 students. However, even with the terrible turnout, Jeff and Tessa gave the audience 110%, and everyone loved it and stayed after to chat with this dynamic duo. Not only do I aspire to be as professional as them, but if everyone was as kind, generous, and genuine as The Evasons, then this world would be a much better place!

We used to do a trick that you've probably seen before where the performer discerns what the audience member has with 5 balls and a bag... 4 balls are one color and the final ball is a different color. People from the audience reach into the bag, remove a ball, hold it in their first, nobody knows who has the odd ball, and yet the performer is able to identify which person that is. We first started doing it as a two person thing where I would have the audience members reach into the bag and I knew who had the odd ball, and I would give that information to Tessa, and she did all the work as far as the presentation goes from the mentalist's point of view. However what I didn't realize when I got that trick was that it involved a magnet and a ring. Now what I didn't realize at the time with the reverse polarity of the magnet was that it really mattered which side was facing which direction when it was in the ring. It could only go in one way for the trick to work 100%, but I didn't realize that. Now in our show we used to offer $100 if Tessa guessed any information wrong. Now we probably did 3 shows where I had to give away $100 before I realized the problem! Now it got to be where I didn't really mind, because it was actually a really good moment to give someone $100. That was almost worth the money right there because it really established that this stuff wasn't 100% and that maybe it wasn't a trick! Although we couldn't rely on the trick, this moment was so powerful so we just left it in the show. However it got to the point where my accountant said you just can't give away a $100... you have to do a check if you're going to write this off as an expense. So I ended up making these little coupons that looked like fake money and I would give it to the person and told them to come up after the show and I would give them a check for accounting purposes. Then after doing this a bunch of times, I realized that due to the reverse polarity, we had to put it in a specific way for it to always work! It wasn't in the instructions, so that was a learning curve that cost a lot of money. At one point we were at a college where our soon-to-be really good friend, Michael DuBois, was there and this show was the first place it had messed up. I ended up handing the bag to him and his buddy, and I said that if there are any mistakes, everyone will get $100! So there was a mistake! I ended up rewriting the script so it turned back into only one person getting $100. Anyway, Michael came up backstage and asked about his $100 and I quickly explained that not everyone gets it, only the person who Tessa guessed wrong and he said "oh okay, that makes sense... I didn't expect you would give out $500!" So then we were very careful about how we worded that trick. I don't think we could have done anything in regards to the reverse polarity, but one thing we did learn from that was to be careful with how you phrase your sentences onstage, because you may have to pay a lot of money!

I remember once we were doing a showcase for NACA (a college campus conference) and I was backstage and Jeff was onstage and we were doing this bit relating to

ghosts and one portion of that was where a Poltergeist Box was set up on this table and what was supposed to happen is that a cloth would fall and the table would shake and we would progress from there to the rest of the routine. It was really very effective and very scary for people. So I was offstage operating this remote, and once the cloth fell I would press the button after counting to three the table would shake. However, at this showcase, the cloth just didn't fall. I could barely see, and since I didn't want the audience to see me I was waiting for Jeff to say something before I hit the button. I never hit it, so Jeff had to just go ahead and wrap it up. Afterwards he asked me why I didn't hit the button, and I realized I was so set on how it was supposed to be that it ended up not looking so great in the end.

Being nice to everyone that you meet, especially in business, is something that I didn't always understand. Especially starting out early in your career, things don't always go according to plan and it took us a while to learn that we must always have a rider- a technical rider. You would think that everything you request would be provided because you've made it sound that it's absolutely necessary. But it doesn't always work out that way, especially in colleges which is about 50% of our work. There will be shows when the students running it will do a poor job of promoting it and there will be hardly anyone there! And that's pretty frustrating when you're providing posters and telling them what to do! However, even with a show where hardly anyone shows up, we still leave with great vibes between us and them. You have to. And not only with the people hiring you! It's the matre'ds, the waiters, all the staff from the top to the bottom. Be nice to everyone and it's only going to come back to bite you if you're not. You can't just rail on people even if it's justified, because it will just get retold and it's a very small world and word spreads to fast. **We try to have a positive attitude from the moment we arrive onsite because you never know from even where you park who you're talking to. We have had a couple instances where even when we're performing at venues where many events are happening, the people that we just happen to bump into turn out to be in our audience. We realize that if we had told them in that moment really how we felt, it wouldn't be good and that would have made an audience member who would be against us.** Once we were driving to a show where there was this real idiot on the highway who just kept passing people and speeding up and slowing down and I probably drove by and who knows what I did because I was in my twenties, but we get to the show and he was in the audience! So it's not always easy, but just be nice to everyone you come in contact with.

When we lived in Canada long ago we did a corporate event in Mexico for a big Shell company. They hired a few magicians to come down. David Ben was on the show, and another really good friend and comedy magician, Mike Carbone, was there too. We ended up going down for the event and Mike Carbone and Tessa and I stayed there for a few days and just hung out in Mexico for a week having fun. By the end of the week it's inevitable that we're all talking with that Spanish/Latin accent. Even after we got back, a few times a week we would call each other just to talk but he would always call and speak into the phone in a heavy Spanish accent- "Hello Mr. Evason!"- and he would have this strong accent. Now one morning, and this was before caller ID, I answer the phone in the morning and the other end opens with "Hello Mr. Evason!" in the strong accent. And I respond in the same strong accent saying "Hello Mr. Carbone, how are you today?" But it turns out it wasn't him... it was a Spanish agent calling for a booking! So now he's all confused on the other end. So I realized that this wasn't Mike, so I continue in the same accent saying "Oh it's Mr. Evason that you want, hold on please" and I put the phone on hold and then I came back on (changing my voice a little bit) and I introduce myself as me! I don't know if I ever fooled him or not, but the booking went through! So always answer the phone professionally, and that's not easy these days because we get so many automated robo-calls and sometimes you just want to answer the phone like "WHAT?!!?" but it's important to remain professional at all times. **Be organized. Have lists- a list of props, list of set, list of tech needs, etc. This includes planning ahead. If you're having a bunch of sound needs or light needs, make sure you get in contact with that person who is running the tech, who may not be the client. This helps out so much so that when you get on site, you won't have the challenges you might think**

unexpectedly. And of course, always be early. I see so many of my friends on Facebook, who are really good acts, and on their personal page they'll talk about how bad the sound system was one night, or how poorly the room was set up or God knows what is working against them. It always makes me wonder why this happens after so many times that they haven't learned to call the venue, or get in contact with the people who are responsible for whatever that is!

You know, it's gotten to the point where people are just going to shows and seeing things and thinking that they can take them as their own. I always think that if you just reach out to people and ask, probably more times than not, people will be happy to let you use a bit or use a joke. And if they don't want you to do it, than just don't do it! Bill Herz (another magician included in this book) is a perfect example- he does this Magic Square and he has a beautiful line that he lets me use! Now Bill is great- he has no ego but all I had to do was ask. I think that people need to know that just because it's out there doesn't mean it's public domain.

There's been a handful of mentors along the way, and if I start naming people I'm sure I'll leave someone out! But I really think that mentors are so important. I see this being talked about (Magic Magazine did a little thing about mentorship in their last issue that we were lucky enough to be a part of) but I think that the best thing we've ever done was when we began to take this seriously and we connected with another act who inspired us to do what we do. Without them I don't think we would be near where we are today and we definitely wouldn't be doing what we're doing today. **There's a couple of other mentors that helped us in other ways, like dance classes! I told the dance teacher what I was doing with Jeff and about the work that we were doing. He told us to come to a couple of dance lessons and he taught us how to move and how to better our physical communication with each other that really helps us with our performance. We had another gentleman who helped us with our verbiage so we wouldn't be repeating lines and so we would be really conscious with our characters and what they are trying to portray. So when Jeff was saying that there were many different mentors, there really were and each one really helped create a viable part to our performance.**

A lot of those mentors, not all of them, come because of our association with the PEA- Psychic Entertainers Association. It's to mentalism what the IBM is to Magic. It encompasses more than just mentalists- psychic readers, hypnotists, so it's all that genre of psychic entertainment. But because of our involvement with that, we've been members for over 20 years, we have met so many great people and have been able to be part of so many great lectures and presentations. It's one of the best things that has ever happened to us, just being in the PEA. Most of the top pros, from Derren Brown to everybody, are in the PEA, along with people that aren't well known but still have a lot to offer. **People there will share information that they normally wouldn't share anywhere else. They save a lot of that** information for an exclusive lecture with no documentation that is only available to members of the PEA. It all boils down to networking! If there's one thing that maybe we could have done more of is just to ask people, and get to know people. I don't do it as much as I should, but you should get to know people and just ask for what you want because usually others love to help

Don't pick drunk people to come onstage! We used to do an Owen's Floating Table... it wasn't like a zombie, it just floated from your fingertips and was used for the spiritual table tipping thing. The table is very simple, and before we would do it we would have the table inspected, and I picked a woman who seemed like she would be great onstage but turned out to be drunk, and she sat on the table and ended up putting a big crack in it! You can't always pick the right people, but the more you do it the more you're able to recognize who's right and who's wrong.

The mistake that I remember most happened when I chose a gentleman who was a bit further from the stage and I asked if he could stand up. I asked someone else to stand up after him, and then I came back to the first guy and asked him to stand up again because I couldn't see him. He was saying something that I couldn't hear so I asked him to repeat himself and he ended up saying "I would stand up if I could stand up, but I'm actually in a wheelchair!" So what I learned is to always walk around the audience to see the scenario. Luckily this gentleman

handled it beautifully and he laughed and the show kept moving.

Along those lines last year we were on a cruise ship in the Caribbean and on this ship it was maybe 50% Canadians. During the show I go into the audience when Tessa is blindfolded and she's identifying spectators objects (see The Evason's appearance on Penn and Teller: Fool Us to watch this awesome routine). I usually can't go into the balcony because that would take away from the flow and most of the audience wouldn't be able to see me, but on this ship they had a horseshoe shaped balcony and on either side of the stage there was a staircase connecting the balcony to the stage. Halfway up the stairs there was a little landing where a few people could stand that everyone in the theater could see. It's a very good visual point. I thought rather than leave everyone out in the balcony, I would go to a person who had an interesting object and asked him to meet me on the landing. It usually worked beautifully but this one night there was a fellow who met me halfway who had a card that he wanted Tessa to identify. The card said "I have a terminal illness, do not resuscitate." There was just no way I could bring this into the show and take it down to that sad level. I whispered to the guy (so that audience couldn't hear) to pull something else out of his wallet. He starts explaining to me, with no voice, that he can't speak- he's pointing to his throat, he doesn't have a voice. His wife came down from the top of the stairs and says to me that he has throat cancer and he's dying and can't talk! So in my microphone I said "I'm so sorry sir, I don't speak French, but come up to us after!" It was the only way I could think of of how to get out of that, and luckily nobody knew! We did see the guy around after and did something to him, but again it's one of those things that you can't foresee ever happening.

Another one of those moments where I'm just like "what's going on?" happened again when I was blindfolded. Jeff had just gone off mic completely, and usually I'm talking to him, but he wasn't coming back on mic to answer. People started laughing, but I couldn't see so I just figured that I would let whatever's happening happen and just go on with the show. He eventually went back on mic and we went on with the show. Now during this particular part of the show Jeff is running around quickly to different people and leaning over people on the aisle seats to interact with people towards the middle of the section. However, suddenly he realizes that there's a young woman who just seemed to be hanging onto him and following him, and he told her that he'll get to her in a minute, even though it seemed as if she was right on top of him! He eventually stopped and realized why she was so close to him. She had long hair and I guess I brushed up against her and her hair ended up getting caught and tangled in the button of my blazer jacket! I was actually dragging her around the audience!

"Don't be scared of failure. Instead, welcome it and let it be your friend. Because after all, friends help each other grow and become better."
-Jake Beinstein

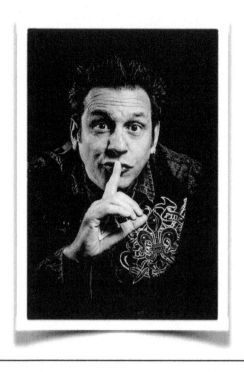

Shawn Farquhar is more than a world champion of magic... he is a two time world champion of magic! He has won the Grand Prix at FISM, Stage Magician of the Year AND Sleight of Hand Magician of the year from the IBM, Magician of the Year by the Canadian Association of Magicians in 2003 and 2010, as well as the Grand Prix D'Honneur by the Pacific Coast Association of Magicians. You may recognize Shawn from his numerous performances and lectures at magic conventions worldwide, or from the not one, but two times he was on *Penn and Teller: Fool Us*! He is a favorite on Disney Cruise Lines and he is constantly traveling to and from exotic destinations around the world to entertain thousands of audiences. The original magic effects he's released have taken the magic community by storm and I highly suggest you check them out.

Man, I have made so many mistakes! Professionally, in the beginning, when I had the branch of my career between the

corporate side and the kids' side- I started as a kids magician and then moved more toward the corporate, comedy clubs, and then into cruise ships- the biggest mistake was not defining who I was early by making a character name. I might have been something else, had I made up a character name (like a Silly Billy, or a Freddy Fusion), I could still be making a ton of money by doing something like selling that character. Because I built up such a huge following as a kids' performer, there was a ton of money coming in! At that time, the 80s, I was making $150 for a birthday party, which was a lot of money back then. And I was doing 4 or 5 on a weekend, and a couple during the weekdays! So I was giving up thirty, forty thousand dollars the day I stopped being Shawn Farquhar, the kids' magician, because I couldn't go out and do a corporate gig for $500-600 at the time for forty minutes, and then say I would do an hour as a kids' entertainer for $150. But if I had two different names and two different looks, I could have made a lot more money and built it up and when I decided to let go of the kids entertainer, I could have probably sold the name and the material, or even just helped another young magician by being the new one! Instead, I just had to let it go, and it was like throwing away an annual income for many people. I had to walk away and start at a lower level in the corporate world in order to try and build it myself.

Late in life I learned that not everyone's going to like me. Originally I thought that everyone would like me, and I wanted everyone to love me- my character, my personality, and who I am is someone who wants to be liked. I grew up on the road, being dropped into different schools all the time and trying to be friends with everybody. I wanted to be that act, that person, the one everybody liked. But the fact is- not everyone is going to like my magic and not everyone is going to like my personality. Learning that lesson and accepting it was probably the hardest thing for me. I thought everybody loved magic as much as I did, but there are people who don't like magic at all! They find it insulting to their intelligence, or it's against their religious beliefs, or they just think it's childish. I had a hard time wrapping my head around that, and so learning to like myself and not care what other people thought about me was probably the biggest life lesson I ever had.

Today when I run into people who maybe think magic is childish, I always try to accept the challenge and try to change their minds, but I don't do it to the point where it's frustrating. If they're not going to accept me, then I move on. The other night there were four people in the room, three of them were die hard fans of magic, begging me to do something and they asked me to do something to the fourth person who I could see had no interest in what I was doing. In fact, he was texting while I was presenting. I asked him to pick a card and he looked at me and asked "do I have to?" and I said "no, actually, you don't!" The other three people then told him to give me his phone so I could show him something with it, and I said only if he wants to, to which he responded, "no, I'd rather keep it" and I said "I totally get it!" There will be people that just don't care, who have no reason whatsoever to think that magic is important.

Be yourself! I spent the first twenty-five years of my career trying to be Mandrake the Magician, David Copperfield, Lance Burton, and all these guys, but when I stopped that and became me, that's when I became successful. I want to tell everybody to find who you are, embrace it, maybe amplify it a little when you're onstage, but try to be true to who you are and don't try to copy somebody. Nobody will ever be as good a copy as you are to you.

I learned this when on a cruise ship doing my act with a pencil mustache and a suave tuxedo, trying to look cool. By the way, if you google 'Shawn Farquhar and Mandrake the Magician" you'll find a picture of me floating a woman, and I've got a top hat and mustache, tuxedo. Frightening!* I did this one show on a cruise by chance- it was my night off. My wife and I went into Rome, we had a bottle of wine, walked in the hot Italian sun, and came back to find out the juggler had hurt himself and we had to do the show! And it was not a good show, because I was drunk and tired. I sat down about halfway through the show, apologized to the audience, and began to just talk to them like they were friends! They responded better than they ever did when I was doing my usual show! I had two shows that night, and during the second show I was more sober. I kind of Hollywooded up what I did in the first show, but it tanked. I realized if I just stayed true to me, it would get better results, and I tried this over the course of the month on the ship. It got to the point where I was just talking to the audience and it became my show now. But it was not by choice, it was by chance, and I'm really glad I discovered it.

Probably the most crucial thing to me are mentors. Not just one, but having many mentors. And not just magic mentors- business mentors! I was fortunate enough to know a man named Gary Switlo- and he had a nickname: The TicketMaster. He had a small company you might have heard of... yea, that's the guy! (If you haven't guessed it, Gary founded TicketMaster). He was phenomenal- he treated me like I was a success decades before I was a success. The way he talked to me and treated me made me feel successful when I was living on ketchup stew.

I have mentors, I have Calvin, who is the guy on the financial side of my world who's helped me in so many ways. And then magicians who you've never heard of, but who were really instrumental in shaping my work ethic and my performance style. Others, like Jerry Andrus, really instilled in me the creativity and the honesty. Mentorship is truly the greatest, and I try to do it now with friends. I have young magician friends that I help, and I try to be more than just the "I'll teach you a trick" mentor. One of my young friends is going through a break up so we went out to dinner and talked about social life. Mentorship should be everything from how you conduct your life to how you do your business, to how you are as a person. I think mentorship is dying in the world of magic. Everybody thinks mentor means "oh, I'll grab somebody young and teach them a trick", but mentors don't always have to be older. I still look for mentors! I have a mentor- this business guy in Malaysia- who's in his thirties, and I learn from him every day by listening to what he's doing and he surrounds himself with mentors. It's about having people with different experiences who are experts, who are willing to share with you and are able to tell you that what they say isn't 100% the truth, but it's 100% their truth. I'm a student! I'm always surprised when people say that they're a 'Master Magician', because I'm an amateur! If you look in my iPhone right now, you'll find like ten videos of guys who showed me tricks in the last month that I want to learn because they just totally fooled me! It was 3 in the morning at the FFFF magic convention and a guy showed me a trick and I was jumping up and down asking him to do it again and he looked at me and was like "Really?! You're the world champion!" And I said "I was the world champion, but now I'm just Shawn and you're freaking me out!"

In 2006 I was standing in front of 3000 of my magic peers at the World Championship of Magic in the finals, broadcast for the BBC television for the close up competition. I was doing my signed card in sealed deck (you can see it on Ellen and Penn & Teller: Fool Us) and I had done well in the preliminaries, so I was pretty sure I was golden. I picked Marc DeSouza, an American magician, out of the crowd to be my volunteer so I had somebody who spoke English, who was familiar with me, and who made me feel comfortable onstage. I had him pick a card, he picked the right card, I had him sign the card, he put it back, he had the deck sealed in his hands, and when I opened the deck and dropped the cards out onto his hands so I could reveal the ending, for some odd reason, the signed card just stayed in the box. I have never been able to repeat it, and my only guess is that the deck had warped on the plane, and because it's one card going into a different deck, the two decks warped in different directions, so when I got the cards out it just sat in the box. Now I didn't see it! The cards fell into Marc's hands, as I was closing back up the box, and talking to Marc, Marc looked down and saw the card in the box and he gave me these eyes like "LOOK!" He kind of nodded his head and I looked down and saw a card in the box! There was a camera directly above pointing down which saw everything, and I right there said to myself "hey! I'm going to lose!" While there were a ton of magicians looking at the giant screen, I snuck the card out and added it to the stack, finished the trick, and ended up doing reasonably well, but not what it was supposed to be, and got second prize. My biggest take away was having learned to not fly with your cards in your checked baggage. Always carry them on the plane with you because the pressure in the cabin is different than the pressure under the plane. So I always travel now with about eight decks of cards in my backpack. I also learned that rehearsal is important! Even when you think you've rehearsed enough, rehearse a little bit more. I suspected if I had rehearsed that day again, maybe I would have seen that problem. I also learned that no matter how much preparation you have, shit happens! I don't care what you do, I don't care how much you practice, something will happen.

It was John Lennon who said "life is what happens while you are busy making other plans." People don't usually address mistakes, people usually hide their mistakes, but I embrace them! I consider them badges of honor! Henry Ford said that each time he made a mistake, he was one step closer to the solution. For me, every mistake I made meant I was one step closer to success!

Below is a picture of Shawn as Mandrake. Yes, it really is him!

Harrison Greenbaum is hands down the funniest guy I know. If you've never seen him, put this book down and check him out on YouTube. When you get back I'm pretty sure he will be the new funniest guy you know! He is also the hardest working guy in the business. At the time of writing this, the calendar on his website says that this month he has 66 shows. 66 shows!! Dead serious. He has appeared on *Last Comic Standing, America's Got Talent,* as well as *Brain Games.* When he's not taking the comedy clubs of New York by storm, he can be seen at prestigious venues across the country such as The Kennedy Center in Washington DC and The Magic Castle in Hollywood. He's got such a strong drive, and chatting with him always inspires me. I hope his contribution will do the same for you.

When I moved to New York City and I was doing stand-up, I wanted to be seen by the industry really fast. I tried to immediately hustle- try out for Comedy Central and all these shows. Every time I meet a new performer I tell them that they're going to make this mistake, but I'm just going to warn them about it. So, here's the warning, but I know you're going to ignore it! This industry will always be there, and the people that will put you on these TV shows and all that stuff will always be there. If it's a show that you want to do right now but you're worried that it might go off the air, don't worry because there'll always be another show and you're better off performing in front of these people and auditioning for them and having them go "holy crap how did we miss this person, this guy is amazing!" as opposed to be "oh yea, in a few years he might be good for the show." I knew a comic who was in Chicago for a really long time, and just got stupidly good. After a while, he finally moved to New York and immediately exploded because everyone thought "holy crap, this guy is ridiculous!" That guy is Hannibal Buress. He came to New York and exploded, because he was undeniably good. So that's the biggest mistake I made- where you try to get to these big auditions right off the bat- whether it's America's Got Talent, or whatever show you want to be on- everyone tries and pushes to get on it ASAP. And even if you do get the show, it's still maybe not the best thing, because if you are able to get the opportunity and exposure, you really want to just knock it out of the park. But then I could say the opposite- an equally dangerous mistake is not taking risks. So you have to balance that out. For my one man show, I've been working on it for a very long time. But here is one of the things I'm glad I did was when I was working on it... I booked a date for the show a few months in the future when I knew the show would be getting to a good place, and I booked it knowing it would force me to finish it. So, basically the moral is, once you know you're ready, it's time to take the jump.

My parents are awesome, and my dad always taught me to be able to wake up and look at yourself in the mirror and be proud of what you've done and know you've done the right thing. There are people who do the wrong thing and they get ahead and it's frustrating. The world is not fair! But the thing that balances it out is waking up and knowing you're doing the right thing. Regardless of your career, knowing you did the right thing, and helping others, is the most important thing. Yes, it's a selfish career being a performer- you're getting up in front of thousands of people saying "look at me, look at me", but it's really important to remember that you're doing this because you want to make other people happy. This is a service job- you're there to help other people. Taylor Swift had a good piece of advice- there's a difference between going onstage and saying to yourself "they're all here to see me" versus going on stage and thinking "I am here to make them all happy." That's a big difference.

This next piece of advice works for all entertainers, and I think in magic it's especially failing, but you've got to be unique and find your voice. As an entertainer, you have to realize that these people are making a big commitment to come see you perform. They're committing time, energy, focus, money- they're making a sacrifice to see you, so you've got to justify that and you have to give them something that is worth their investment. This usually means being original and creative, it means talking about things that are worth talking about, and it all comes from this place of doing the best possible job you can do and being truly you. A lot of entertainers, especially in magic, are doing a lot of the same stuff as each other but the key is finding out who you are and making each thing you do uniquely suited to you.

If you want a really good show, there should be a story of how every trick went wrong in every single way. Basically, anytime a trick goes well in my act, it's because I've earned that by screwing it up every way that was possible before. So every trick in my show has a thousand stories of how it went wrong. Every audience is a new experience! There is no constant. So you always have new, weird things that you have to deal with. One of the crazier ones happened to me in Gloversville, New York. Gloversville is called Gloversville because they used to have a glove factory, but then China started making gloves much cheaper so now they're just sad and gloveless. This is the town, they're small, and in the Adirondacks so you have to take a train there. It's the kind of town that has the town gay! Like he's married with children, but everyone knows... I met him- they were very hasty to introduce me to him! He was delightful. The show happened to be in an old tiny movie theater that looked beautiful on the outside, but they completely gutted the inside of it so there's just folding chairs and the remains of the theatre- very much like an empty void inside.

I'm doing my show- it was a long show- I was the headliner and was scheduled to do 45 minutes. This is the second year I had done the show and the turnout wasn't as good as the first year, and it was a very dark room, but as soon as I hit the stage I can see that there is a guy who's asleep. An old guy with a white moustache who is definitely asleep. He's kind of leaning on whoever he came with. So I start with my set and I know that 40 minutes in, I'm going to go into the Baby Trick, because that's 5 minutes, and it's my closer. As I'm starting the Baby Trick, because I know it's my big closer, I look back at the guy and ask if someone can poke that guy to make sure he's alive, and everyone laughs. Someone pokes him, and he literally goes from leaning over to upright- he jerks upright and yells "FAGGOT!" and then he throws a beer bottle at me! He misses- he misses by a lot- but the weird part is as far as I know, he was sleeping throughout my entire show. He has no idea what I'm talking about onstage. So for all I know, that is how he wakes up! That's just how he always wakes up, every morning- he yells a slur and throws a beer bottle- like that's just who he is! And the weird part is that it's a small town where everyone knows each other. So almost the whole town is at the show, and afterwards everyone comes up and tells me not to worry because they're going to make it real awkward for him.

Another time I was at a Comedy Club where the act before me was really antagonizing an audience member, but I was working on my set offstage so I didn't really fully take it in, but he was just going after him and going after him. I get onstage and his girlfriend gets up to go to the bathroom. I make a little joke about her going to use the bathroom when I got onstage and her boyfriend, who had probably been building up his anger, stands up and pushes me, then stands up and gets onstage and pushes me again, really aggressively! At that point the owner of the club gets up onstage and wrestles him off. The whole audience was just like "holy crap!" For my first line I looked over at the owner and said "you recorded this one, right?" He said "nope", so I said "let's bring him back, we're doing it again for YouTube!" The weird part was after five minutes of doing damage control (because that was during the 45 minute set I was booked to do), I had to keep going and I got the crowd back, but then the girlfriend got back from the bathroom... she had no idea that any of this had transpired! So I told her that she might want to go outside and call her boyfriend, and that was interesting to see her running out going "oh shit"!

Many of the magicians included in this book have spoken about how important mentors are in their lives. I am so incredibly lucky to be able to call **Bill Herz** my mentor. He has taught me to be a better magician, a better businessman, and most importantly- a better person. Bill is probably one of the most influential magicians who you've never heard of. When he's not performing in his own 150+ corporate events a year, he produces and manages Michael Carbonaro's tour and represents the best names in magic- David Copperfield, Mac King, Derren Brown, Derek Hughes, Rob Zabrecky, Jon Stetson, David Williamson, and many others who are fortunate enough to be on his roster. All of these performers will attest that Bill is one of the best guys in the business.

Onstage, the biggest mistake I've made is not knowing who my audience is before I went onstage, as well as thinking that every audience is the same. You've got factors that you have to take into account- are you in a restaurant or a bar, what's the mood of the audience, etc. For me, since I'm all corporate, the big thing is that if they've been sitting all day in meetings, how do I make sure the stuff I'm going to do isn't taking too much concentration at the beginning, because they're tired. I know I have to get them on my side right away- I can't open with a mentalism routine that takes a lot of thought on their part to get them involved. It's really important to know who they are and grab them at the beginning when you can.

Business-wise, my biggest mistake would have to be rushing into trying new things. Not necessarily tricks, but new ways to market and new ways to reach my potential clients. I've probably wasted a lot of money and time by not really examining beforehand what I'm about to do and by not doing my market research. For example, recently I did a direct mail thing. Well, the open rate was not as successful as I would have liked... I should have tested it out a bit more. But I learned that the next time I try direct mail, I have to look into the timing and the receiver- what time of year, how far in advance I'm trying to get them to buy, am I hitting the right people (people always think that meeting planners are the ones who buy talent- they're not. It's usually the marketing manager or the communications manager).

You're in trouble if you believe your own press. If you believe what others say positively (ie "you're the best!"), you're in trouble. We all hear "oh my God, you're the most amazing magician I've ever seen!" and we believe it, because we hear it fifty times a night. But the truth of the matter is every magician is hearing that every night. If you're not hearing it, something's wrong! The problems come when you start believing it.

Work. There is nothing that replaces work. Think about a restaurant. If I told you I read every book on running a restaurant I could believe that I know everything there is to know about running a restaurant. But it all changes completely when you start actually running a restaurant- all of the theory goes out the window for practicality. Same thing for performing! Every successful performer I know has paid their dues (performing everywhere and anywhere)... there is no way around it. None. It's hard, but it's so important to find a place to be bad. Whether it be the street or a restaurant, a place where they'll let you do 7 or 8 minutes onstage every night, comedy clubs, whatever! You have to find a place to be bad because there is no way you're going to learn otherwise. You should be working as much as you can.

Once I inadvertently used a joke that backfired in an embarrassing way. It was horrible and the audience hated me. I was performing for a large group in Arizona- a jam-packed room. I asked for a volunteer and I saw a woman wearing a very flowery shirt on. I couldn't see her, I just saw her arm and I said "by the way, that's a beautiful blouse, who shot the couch?" It's an old joke, that always gets a laugh. But tonight, she stood up and weighed probably 450 pounds. The whole audience had thought that I had just called her a couch. They hated me after that! I didn't cover... I went on with the show but they thought I had called someone fat, which of course I would never do.

I remember buying the trick 'Mother of All Book Tests' a few years ago, and while performing it, turned around. With my back turned, the guy 'helping' me started ripping the pages out, thinking it was a normal book. I remember freaking out because it was an $800 book at the time!

Be prepared for everything that can go wrong, and have a game plan for when this happens, or this doesn't happen, or whatever it might be, have contingency plans.
This preparedness is crucial. In fact, when looking for performers to represent and book, I look to make sure of a few things:
• They've worked in every situation
• No whining!
• Can do a commando performance (anywhere, anytime).
• People who are flexible
• No ego
• People who know what's going in the world- people who are aware
so they can converse easily with the clients.
• They have to be really entertaining- not just technically good, but

really entertaining.

My favorite prank was probably on Chad Long- we almost made him buy a new tuxedo. I can't go into the full story, but he thought he was underdressed so we convinced him to go out and buy a tuxedo. We stopped him at the last minute. There are so many pranks! We put a chicken in David Williamson's hotel room, when we were at this real country-type inn. But he was really smart- he didn't show any response! I nailed Derek DelGaudio and Jason England at the same time, convincing them I had sold them for a corporate event to do some incredible dealing, and then told them that it had to be with a beat up old deck... they freaked!

"If you live long enough, you'll make mistakes. But if you learn from them, you'll be a better person. The main thing is never quit, never quit, never quit."
-President Bill Clinton

In 2014 when **Jeff Hobson** was playing on Broadway with The Illusionists, I sent him an email asking if I could meet him after the show. Despite the fact that he had no clue who I was, he was gracious enough to go out to dinner with me and a friend of mine after the matinee performance, and then took us backstage before the show that evening! He is considered "The Host of Las Vegas", having appeared in shows up and down the Strip. He is a favorite of many Fortune 500 companies and his talents have been seen on HBO, Showtime, Fox, and NBC. In 2010 he won Stage Magician of the Year by the Academy of Magical Arts, which added to his long list of awards and honors. He is one of the funniest men in the business, and when it comes to character development, this man has it mastered it.

There's a couple of stories that haunt me, that I keep on re- living and am embarrassed about. The first was when I was working my first "real" professional gig in Detroit when I was about twenty. That's when I was working at Mr. F's (Mr. Furtney's Beef and Bourbon) in Michigan... it was the last of the traditional night clubs in town. So it had a small stage, a small bandstand behind the stage, and was surrounded by people who were eating on multi-tiered platforms so everyone could see you, even though you're standing on the floor. In my earlier days I was much more brash and not quite as smart as I am now. One of those things that I remember growing up in the comedy club era of the 80's was when performers would ask audience members "hey, how are ya?", "where're ya from?", "what do you do for a living?", just to get conversation going and to make jokes on their behalf, which was a thing that everybody did in those days that I tried to take and put into my act. In this club, which was the worst kind of situation for magicians because people were eating, most of them with your backs towards you, I had to perform a show. So I would go up to people and ask them the questions, and make fun of them, doing like a Don Rickles thing. That was sort of accepted at the time of being the norm, so I wasn't really insulting anybody, and pretty much everyone could take a joke in those days... except for when you go a little bit too far. One of the shows I saw this lady who was pregnant! It really looked like she was nine months pregnant. And I reached my mic down to her as I said "hey, how long have you been knocked up?" I put the mic in her face and she looked up from her plate and she coldly replied "I'm not pregnant." So I just pretty much erased my career at that point!

A more important mistake which was during that same time of my life happened when I was working at the Canadian National Exhibition in Toronto which was a twenty-one day fair at the time. I would do about ten shows a day and each of those shows I would perform the linking rings, because that's what I was requested to do. So I'm performing the linking rings ten times a day for twenty-one days straight. This is the twenty-first day and I'm pretty much tired of the linking rings at this point- I really started to hate the trick! I'm doing the show at one of the pavilions and there's about two thousand people in the crowd- it's an outdoor show. Now at this point I don't care who I get up or what I'm doing, I just want to go home and get back to Michigan where I was from. So I brought these two kids up, and I didn't even care who they were, I just pointed to two kids haphazardly, and they came up onstage. I got my linking rings out of the box, I turned back around and saw that one of the kids was standing on my left side and one was standing on my right. A girl on my left, a boy on my right, and we were all facing the audience. So I'm going through the trick and I say "here, hold onto these rings" to the girl on my left, and then I say to the boy on my right "hold out your hand". Now he's standing on my right side and he holds up his left hand. Then of course the traditional whole hack line that I used was "no, no, no, the clean one!" Well as he turns his body I notice that he had an atrophy paw of about two fingers sticking out of his shoulder. So he turns his body and showed the two little fingers to the audience and pretty much my throat went back into my stomach and I continued on with the trick, but ever since then, the haunting of those two instances make me relive those horrible moments even decades later as being just the worst times that I ever felt. Today I'm very, very careful and very very courteous to people I bring onstage and that before I say any line to them I make sure that it's not going to offend them like those lines back then did.

The best life lesson I was ever taught is something that I think I knew inherently and was common sense. Treat everyone with respect the first time you meet them, because you never know who those people are or what they do. I really learned this during the one month of my career when I actually had a regular job selling cars. I had this old man come up to me, all hunched over at the car dealership and somebody told me that this man might want to buy a car. Well, I looked at him and he looked poor, ragged, bent over, and maybe 90 years old. I just thought that I would pass him onto another salesman because I don't have any time for this guy because he doesn't look like he wants to buy a car and who wants to deal with an old, slow, cranky guy with probably no money. Well within about a half an hour I see him sitting down at the table with the other salesman and this guy takes rolls of money out of his pocket and pays for his car in cash! Ever since that moment I learned that you can't prejudge people and you have to treat everyone with respect right off the bat as soon as you meet them.

The most important advice I can give to people, especially people who are starting out, I say that no matter what you know now, or what you want to know in magic, wait until your 500th performance, and after 500 shows you won't have any more questions. Just perform as often as you can. I don't know where I pulled the 500 out but I think it was in my teen years when I did over 500 shows, because I was one of the busiest teen magicians in Detroit, and probably by the time I was nineteen or twenty I had performed at least 500 shows, and I pretty much had a lot of questions when I started magic and after that many many shows you'll probably know most things you need to know about performing. So keep performing and keep getting on stage! Even if it's in shows at school, or to introduce somebody, even if it's just to get up in front of people and tell a joke, whatever it is, the more experience that you have in front of people talking publicly, is the best thing you can do for your career as an entertainer.

Looking back, I would have dropped the conformity that magicians fall into sooner. Many of us are still caught up in the 1800s mentality of dressing a certain way, using certain props that don't fit in, and all the way up until the 1980s when I was in my twenties, I was still wearing tuxedos and had a preconceived idea of what magicians should look like onstage and I think I could have dropped that sooner and not gone the traditional route of magic. I think that would have spawned more creativity earlier.

The only resource I had growing up were books- I cherished them. The reason why some of the old phonies in magic (and I think I'm falling into that category!) say "don't watch the videos, yadda yadda ya", and the only reason why I think that books are important is because the book forces you to take your time and absorb information on a slower, more even basis than watching a few minute video that "teaches" you quickly. It's sort of like what radio did as opposed to television. Radio shows, when they first started, forced you to be creative and imaginative. Say it was a cowboy show, all listeners would perceive it in different ways. They would see different colors in the cowboy's outfit, they would perceive the landscape differently, etc. Yet when you get to television it stripped away most of that creativity. The scripting was hard, the costumes were a certain color, people acted a certain way, and it stripped away your own creativity and you're at the mercy of whoever's acting and directing. I think that's what's happening with a lot of magic videos today- I think creativity is a bit stifled because we see something and that's the way we believe it has to be performed. Whereas if you were to read something, like a method to a trick without the exact presentation, you're forced to be creative!

If you're a magician, chances are you own and use religiously one of **Joshua Jay**'s best selling products, of which there are too many to list. My first encounter with Josh was when I was in eighth grade and I sent him an email asking him if he would come to my assembly of the Society of Young Magicians and lecture and he agreed. Getting to talk with him before and after his lecture (which was absolutely incredible) proved to me that he was one of the nicest magicians I've ever met. He is the co-founder of my go-to magic shop, the online mecca of Vanishing Inc. What separates Vanishing Inc. from all the other magic suppliers is that they only sell products that are proven to be solid pieces of magic. They don't stock something just because it's new, but because it's a powerful piece that audiences will love. Pretty much all of us have learned from Josh, and hopefully by reading his contribution you'll learn a little bit more than tricks.

There was a point in time, about seven years ago, when I founded Vanishing Inc. and I signed on to write the Jay Sankey books with my friend and business partner, Andi Gladwin. It's not that those books are a mistake, I actually think those books are really great and if anything I think they're overlooked treasures for magicians, but the hundreds and hundreds of hours that I put into those books in my mid-twenties was time, looking back, that I could have spent pursuing my own career, my own shows, and TV appearances. What I think of what those books meant to us as a company and what they did for my career versus how I could have spent that time otherwise, I regret that if I'm being truly candid. However, now I'm at a different time in my career than I was then, and Vanishing Inc. has proven to be very, very worthy of my time and very exciting. I love working on Vanishing Inc. projects more than I enjoy doing shows that don't excite me. But, I also know that shows that do excite me have to take precedent over passive projects because they only come about every so often.

The best life lesson I learned, although corny and pedestrian, is so true and is something I will teach to my future kids someday. When I was pretty young, my dad said that I have to find something that I love and find a way to spend my life doing it. I think that he was speaking from a place of experience and of regret- he had a career that he didn't love doing every day and so I think he wanted the opposite for me. I love magic and it's how I would spend my time if I had to pay to do it, so what a ridiculously cool thing that every single moment of my day is spent developing, performing, and creating magic... it's great!

To people who are new in magic, you've got to love it. I help a lot of young magicians- I spend part of my day in some form- whether it's with the charity that we've created or just individually with the kids who I like and work with. There's kind of a beautiful thing about magic where every kid gets into it because it's cool, and there are some easy tricks that are amazing, but there's this period in the teen years where it gets hard to be a magician. The squeeze is on! The girls, or school work, or whatever it is enters the picture and it gets hard. Social pressures, school pressures, sports, whatever comes up in a kid's life. And it's kind of beautiful because it weeds out the people who don't truly love the art. I always say that the number one rule if you're getting started in magic is you've got to decide if you love it. There's nothing wrong with not loving it to death, but then just know that it's going to be a hobby, like collecting baseball cards or taking tap dance lessons. There's no room in magic for full time professionals who aren't real wild and crazy about magic. I love it to death. All my friends are magicians, all my thoughts are on magic, I read about magic, I watch magic, it's everything to me! There's just no room in magic for people who don't feel that way unless they want to treat it as a hobby, which is great! But that's a very different kind of thing.

For adults, it's hard to give advice because there are so many different paths. I heard people tell me that social media is a waste of time and that nobody books magic through social media, and I watch some things that Rick Lax and Justin Flom have done that blow me away! They're amazing! I heard magicians tell me that there's no future in the magic community, it's too small, there's no money to be made, and that's just not true. I've had magicians tell me that the only way forward is with theatrical shows, one man shows, like when I did "Unreal", so it's clear that there is no one path and there are so many ways to skin the cat. That for me is truly exciting! So I wouldn't want to give anybody any "do or don't" advice because people prove those sorts of advice wrong every day.

Any success I've had on the artistic side of magic is due to the fact that my mom instilled in me a really cool quality which is the ability to be okay with being wrong or being okay with being not great at something. My friends will tell you that I beg them for criticism, that I will purposely show them a trick and insist that they break it apart. I'll send them a clip or I'll have them watch my show and I will push them to find faults to help make me better. I will invite people over, truly every week of my life, to make sure that whatever I'm doing is good with the whole group- people whose opinions I trust, laymen, whoever. I am stunned at how few magicians have that quality. I have just stopped volunteering advice to friends and magicians because it's so clear that they just don't want it! Things are good enough, things are fine the way they are, I've been doing it this way for years/why would I change, and that sort of mentality breathes complacency and mediocrity. That is prevalent in our industry because so few magicians are willing to workshop and hone and work on ideas. I truly believe that the gestation period for a magic trick is forever. But to speak in practical terms, it's years. Years and years and years. If you've seen Mac King, you'll see it in action. Mac is always working on tricks, even ones that have been in his show for years. I'm stunned when the incubation for most magicians I know is weeks, days! At most a month! Then they just sort of go "it's where it's at, it's done, I'm going to release it now, I'm going to put it into my show, etc" and I'm shocked by that. Being able to admit you're wrong is so valuable, and not just in magic, but also in business.

Andi and I have never had a fight and have never raised our voices at each other. It's been seven years, there have been some big decisions, some big problems, some great things, but we've never fought because we both have the ability to go "you were totally right about that" or "I was wrong, let's go back to square one and do this again," and I think that that's what makes the partnership successful and easygoing. We work with a lot of magicians and a lot of magicians come to us. Figuring out who to work with is easy. Step one- they have to be a friend or somebody we are compatible with. We have worked with one too many magicians who are headaches, and we are just more than willing to trade a successful product and some money away for the pleasure of working with people we like. Step two- when it comes to quality of products, the main thing we look for is something that's been tested. Somebody that shows evidence that they've been using this trick, that it's been tried and modified based on audience reaction is something we like. We don't like people that say "here's an idea I came up with, I want to do this, I haven't really tried it, but here's the idea." That sort of thing isn't us. We want something that we can release that magicians can use with confidence because somebody has already road tested it. I've learned a lot by road testing material over my years.

Some of my most embarrassing stories go way back to when I was a kid. When I was a very young magician I was doing an Ohio Power Retiree's Banquet- all these people that work for a power company in Ohio. I was the entertainment, young boy magician Joshua Jay, and the speaker that day was the Governor of Ohio. There's like five hundred people there. I thought it would be clever, in my infinite wisdom, to get the Governor onstage for my hat-tear routine in which I used messed up wands and I made the what was usually a kid volunteer dance around the stage in a ridiculous manner. So I had the Governor onstage dancing around like a monkey with wands between his leg with the crotch jokes, and my dad is watching from the wings just wincing in pain at what an embarrassing miscalculation this is. So embarrassing the Governor wasn't my most shining moment!

Another time later on in my career, I was doing this Chinese coin trick with a ribbon (Charming Chinese Challenge) and once in awhile when I would go to throw the coin and catch it on the ribbon, I would accidentally let go and release the ribbon and the coin would fly out of my hand like a projectile, and one time the coin flew out of my hand and right down a busty woman's dress... like right between the boobs, all the way in! Fortunately it was taken as funny and it was hilarious and everybody laughed, but that could have gone a totally different direction. Another time I was doing it and it went right bullseye in a woman's cup of soup which was not funny.

However, I don't have many horror stories. I would have to attribute that to the fact that I am a neurotic list maker. Before I go out on any stage, I triple check a set up list, I triple check all my props, I am totally neurotic about it. So there have been so many times where ten seconds before going out onstage I've checked a list and realized I forgot to load the lemon with the bill, or something that would have gone horribly wrong BUT I saved myself. I have my own system in my phone, in the notes app, so I can make one for every show I do, but I copy and paste from a master list. Basically there's the trick list which is in running show order, but indented in each trick are all the things that I have to do to set it up. So like I do a ring in M&Ms pack trick and the list will say "Ring to M&Ms", and then in the subcategory it would say "thumb tip in holder with M&Ms inside", "M&Ms opened and modified in holder in case", "ring box prepared with magnet in position", "sharpie in left jacket pocket," all these things so I could go down the list and mentally check everything off. My material is intense- I am not afraid to go very far to prepare things. Because of that, I have a lot more set-up than most magicians. With a lot of guys it's like a source of pride- they say they could do their show out of their briefcase, and there's no set up, and they can walk in the room 20 minutes before, but I'm just not one of those guys. I have to be at the show two hours before, and I have a big checklist and a lot of things I need, but the show I give I'm really proud of! I think my show has got a lot in it that says "wow, this person has put a lot of time into this."

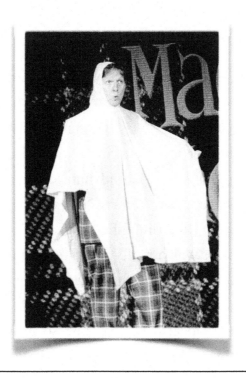

Does **Mac King** even need an introduction? In case you don't know who he is, he holds the title of the longest running magic show in all of Vegas- a stunning 17 years, doing 10 shows a week at Harrah's Hotel and Casino. He was named "Magician of the Year" by the Academy of Magical Arts, he appeared on *The Late Show with David Letterman*, on *Penn and Teller: Fool Us* (twice!), and so much more. In the summer before my senior year of high school, my parents sent their 17 year old son (me) alone to Las Vegas to spend the summer learning from this master. Even after watching 80 some odd shows from backstage, I still laugh at the jokes and am amazed at his incredible demeanor onstage. Even after watching his damn rope trick over 80 times, I still can't figure it out! Getting to learn from Mac was priceless, and I am so grateful for the opportunity.

My grandfather, my mom's dad, was really encouraging for me to pursue magic, or whatever! My parents got divorced when I was younger, so he was kind of a surrogate dad for me. Thinking about this as a parent now, I think it was, in a way, an advantage for me to have him! I think kids have a hard time taking advice from their parents and so having a grandfather give me strong advice and encouragement was a really great thing and I think I had the tendency to listen to him more than I would if it was my dad giving me that same bit of advice. He was just really encouraging, and also he was just so influential in my life. There's not one specific piece of advice he gave me, but there was stuff like "don't burn bridges"- stuff as simple as that. I've had disagreements with people in the past, or they've done stuff I think is wrong or not above-board, but I've never really shut anybody out because of how I felt like I was treated. I'm not saying I'm perfect, I'm sure I was a dick to people too, but that was one of the things he instilled in me. And other things just as simple as "when you're talking to people, look them in the eye, listen to what they have to say!" His advice didn't directly relate to magic, but you can extrapolate it to ideas like when you have someone onstage, don't treat them like a prop! Treat them as a human, look them in the eye, and listen to what they have to say.

The crucial thing for me has been always having someplace to do a bunch of shows. When I was a teenager working at an amusement park doing three shows a day (sometimes as many as six), seven days a week, well that was amazing! And then when I moved onto comedy clubs, doing 7-10 shows a week, that was great too. I have nothing against cruise ships, people would always tell me I should try them out, but I always thought there weren't enough showtimes. You're only doing at most a couple of shows a week. Compared to ten a week, that would take you five times as long to get better! So from Comedy Clubs to Harrah's, it's been 10 shows a week. I've always had someplace to just do shows, and I feel like if you look at the people who do the most shows- David Copperfield has probably done the most shows out of everybody, and he's the best magician alive. And then I would say Penn and Teller or maybe Lance Burton are next. And so you look at this and go "so maybe the people who've done the most shows are the best, it turns out"! And I don't think that's a coincidence. So those three venues- the amusement park when I was a teenager, and then comedy clubs, and then Harrah's, it's been pretty much boom-boom-boom. Those are three places I've worked in my life and they've always had a lot of shows.

Another crucial resource to me is having smart friends. I was really lucky to have met Lance Burton when I was 14. He and I did shows together, and it turns out he's really smart about being a magician! Doing shows with him for three years and seeing how he worked on his magic, how he thought about methods, routining,and how he incorporated moves into natural reactions was great! As I got further along in my career, I made more smart friends and got their input, so that's another resource- magician friends. But the other crucial resource was when I started working in comedy clubs. I would see the headliners and would watch to see how they construct their shows. The guys that were good would record their shows every night, and then spend the next day thinking about the show the night before and figuring out how to make it better. Observing their work ethic and the way they constructed shows was just another great resource. Especially when I became a headliner, this was really invaluable.

Every tiny little thing that can go wrong has gone wrong. The first time I headlined a club on the road was in Denver, Colorado. I was doing the thumb-tie that I still do in my show, and somehow the volunteer actually wired my thumbs together! I didn't do the secret maneuver correctly, and I still don't know exactly what I did wrong, but I was like "shit! I'm really tied up here!" At another comedy club in Dallas, Texas, I'm standing in the back of the room waiting to go on, talking to the middle act before I go up and I don't realize that I've been introduced! So whoever was the middle act told me that I had just been introduced, so I ran to the stage- it was a comedy club stage, but it was like 3 steps up. So I jumped up onto the stage, and I'm wearing dress shoes- leather bottom shoes. My feet slipped out from under me and I went sprawling onto the stage! Now I've got body loads all over me- I have a bottle of beer and a rock, and both of those went shooting across the stage out of their secret holders. So the beer is rolling across the stage, and the rock is rolling the opposite way, and I haven't even done one trick! But two of the big tricks which are towards the end of the show are sitting on the stage. I just picked them up and put them back where they belong and went on the show. They still got a good reaction, but that was awful!

I was living in LA when my wife and I first moved to California, and the one time I took a cruise ship job (I was looking for money!), I was supposed to fly to Japan. I was packing up my bags and I'm putting the plane ticket in my case and I realize that the flight left an hour ago. I had misread the ticket! It was awful. That was probably 25 or 26 years ago, and just thinking about it makes my stomach upset. It was just awful! My wife was in graduate school at the time so she wasn't home then, and I remember running around our little apartment in circles- "OH NO, OH MY GOD, OH NO, OH MY GOD! HOLY FUCK! SHIT!"

But the most important thing is to be a good listener. That's kind of the main piece of advice... it applies in so many situations and I think that people don't do it very much. Take that as broadly as you can- listen to the audience, listen to the person who's onstage with you, listen to yourself, listen to your friends, when you're talking to somebody when you're talking about doing a show in their venue, listen to what they have to say, listen to the light and sound guys, when you're on TV listen to what the producers have to say, listen to the directors, but then again at the end of the day, you have to remember to listen to yourself too.

"Sometimes when you innovate, you make mistakes. It's best to admit them quickly, and get on with improving your other innovations."
-Steve Jobs

In a nutshell, **Jeff McBride** is a three-time Guinness World Record holder, three-time award winner at the Grand Prix of Magic in Monte Carlo, he was voted Best Magician in Las Vegas when headlining 'Caesars Magical Empire', and he has been featured on every major television network. He is the creator and director of The Magic and Mystery School in Las Vegas- a coveted venue where magicians from around the world learn and explore magic. I first met Jeff at a magic convention in 2011 when I was 12. I just starting learning card manipulation from his DVD "Manipulation Without Tears" and I had a couple questions for him. I shyly went up to him at his dealer's booth, and he helped me with what I was having trouble with, while having an encouraging smile on his face. He does so much to help magicians and the magic community as a whole, and I hope that his contribution to this book will help you too.

Looking back, I would have changed my first name to what is now my screen actor's guild name- Magnus. I would have gone with Magnus McBride because it sounds more mythic. It's too late for me to change now, but I think that brand names and magicians names have a powerful impact. A name can enter the room years before the magician does. Jeff was a little too casual for that intense character I created back in the eighties. What I learned from this mistake is how to help others brand themselves. I've worked with a lot of magicians. For instance, I helped Bill Cook change from Bill Koch (his natural name). Your name travels further and wider than you ever will, so it's good to have a strong brand name in magic.

Branding is a big part of what we do at the Magic and Mystery School. We start with the act because there is no way you can market something that is not good. First and foremost we teach good magic. A huge demographic of the magic community are hobbyist, collectors, and enthusiasts who want to deepen their understanding. While we get a lot of these folks, we also get a lot of professionals who come to our school to not only work on their acts, but to work on the business end. Business is the bigger word of show business and a lot of people forget that, which is why marketing, branding, and business are heavily covered at The Mystery School.

Eugene Berger once quoted Tenkai- the Japanese master- who said "Magic is not tricks. It is a way." When I started, I thought that magic was just about tricks and performances. As I studied the history of magic, I saw that it was a much more profound way of living life. There is no life outside of magic. Magic is like being in the Dao for me. There are many that choose to make the distinction between being onstage and being offstage, when they put their props away and when they take them out again, but I believe what Shakespeare said- "All the world's a stage". Magic is not something I can put up or put down. It's something that I am. For me there is no life outside of magic, as magic is my life.

Study with masters. I learned a lot of bad habits as a kid, learning on my own. But my career really took off when I studied with masters. I trained with some of the best performers and sleight of hand artists- Jeff Sheridan was my street magic teacher, Frank Garcia taught me manipulation, Bobby Baxter taught me comedy magic, Eugene Berger taught me the philosophy of magic, and Larry Hass teaches me about the deeper meaning of magic as it relates to the mind of the performer. My Mystery School team is the most crucial resource to me- they're experts in performance, philosophy, psychology, theater, computers, social media, video production, script editing, costuming, music production, prop fabrication, so we have created an extraordinary community of inspired professionals at the top of their game who have collaborated to create this extraordinary experience that we call the Mystery School. It's taken a lifetime and it daily it proves to be a source of inspiration to me, and I hope it can be for others as well.

"The successful man will profit from his mistakes and try again in a different way."
-Dale Carnegie

David Oliver was my first teacher of magic, coming into my life when I was a 7 year old camper at a magic day camp. Over the next decade I got to know David very well at magic conventions, Tannens Magic Camp, various shows and lectures, and visits to his Society of Young Magicians assembly in Boston. He has made his mark as one of the foremost teachers of young magicians, having mentored and taught hundreds of budding conjurers. He is best known for having a double lung transplant, after his original lungs were devastated by dust from doves he would use in his act. Needless to say, the birds have vanished from his repertoire! He is a regular performer at Monday Night Magic, New York's longest running off-Broadway magic show, and entertains at birthdays, banquets, and other private events.

I don't have any regrets in the business because I realize everything I've done has led to who I am as a person and a performer to day. I know that sounds corny, but that's how I feel. As far as mistakes, while I wouldn't say it was a mistake, I should have taken more business courses in college. I should have focused more on the business side of magic when I was younger, learning about investments and retirement, learning how to run a business, because most of that I've had to learn on my own through trial and error. A lot of it took a long time to learn and I did make mistakes with some business things that I probably would have been able to get through faster, easier, and better had I known more. But when I went to college I studied English and theater, thinking that would help me with my performances, not realizing I already had most of the knowledge that I needed for the performance, as it was what I had always done. What I lacked was the knowledge for the business side of it and I should have either found a mentor or taken college courses on the business side of things. As the director of the Society of Young Magicians in Boston, I try to push learning the business side of things onto the young people that I work with... you can learn all the tricks and the magic that you want, but make sure to learn some business stuff too. Some of it starts with teaching them just how to answer the phone and how to talk to clients on the phone, how to be polite on the phone, and just simple things I eventually learned many years ago. Like smiling! Smiling when talking on the phone carries through the airways. People can sense a happy person, especially when you smile on the other end of the phone. I teach the kids how to have a "phone list"- a list with all the questions to ask a client so you don't forget anything (location, timing, etc of the show). Many people will say "oh, let the kids learn it on their own, let them figure it out on their own like we did" but I'm trying to help magic progress by teaching them as much as I can to get them to the next step a little faster than how I got there.

As it has been pointed out by many other people, it's show business and business is the much bigger and important word. For me, the performing side is only about 10% of the time and 90% of my time is the business these day. I enjoy that 10% so much that I will put up with the 90% of business just to do that 10% of performing.

A powerful lesson for me happened at the Society of American Magicians Convention in 1985 in Boston. I had never been to a ational convention, but I saw they had a competition and I thought I was really good so I put together this act which was separate from the usual shows I was doing at birthday parties and blue and gold banquets. I put together what I thought was a special act just for this competition. On the application form I checked off the box for "illusionist" because I thought after all I'm doing illusions! Not illusions as we magicians know it, but I thought the term would make me sound better. I put together a little vignette of a performance with a dancer I knew, and she was helping me out with it. It was set in a restaurant setting and all this magic happened around our restaurant setting with candles appearing and vanishing and things happening and birds appearing and a dancing cane was involved that appeared in midair before it danced. We had the girl vanish and then she's supposed to appear at the end when I pull the tablecloth off the table and hold it up in front of me, and this worked for at least two months of rehearsal every day.

We get to the convention and set up and as we're loading in one of the major props fell out of the back of the car and smashed on the ground and broke. So I had to quickly put together something that was different for that spot in the show because there was no way I could rebuild this prop. So we set up and came the competition time! The room fills with almost a thousand magicians and I'm backstage huffing and puffing, ready to go, my name is called, curtain opens, and there's no music. I'm standing frozen onstage and my girl is standing frozen onstage in her position and there's still no music. I'm waiting, and I'm just about ready to walk offstage and tell them to close the curtains and start again, and I heard somebody call for music, and my music started. I may have only been onstage for four or five seconds but it seemed like three hours. The act started okay, the first couple tricks went well, people clapped, but the first snag came with my bird productions. I was using this new web-like glue that seamstresses and tailors use to hold cloth together. You put it between two pieces of cloth, iron it, and it melts and then re-sticks to the cloth. I figured it was faster than sewing so I put it in my dove pockets! Well, onstage due to the very hot stage lights, this glue started to melt. While I was onstage, I felt the bottom of the pockets melt and the birds slowly started to slide down my belly and my sides. I ended up having to put my arms against them to hold them in place until I did the production. Then the first major error...

The girl was supposed to vanish... she had to sneak out of the costume she was wearing (an overcoat type piece), which worked fine in all the rehearsals. But onstage when she went to go slip out of the costume, a safety pin popped open and gouged her leg as she hit the floor. Blood started squirting everywhere. She fell to the floor, and instead of vanishing I whispered to her to walk offstage like we just had an argument, so she did so with a trail of blood following her (we found out later she needed 17 stitches). I'm now thinking "okay, she's not in the secret compartment for her appearance at the end of the act, so I have no ending. So I'm not in the best of moods and my serious act started to turn into a comedy act. Another prop didn't work, the thread snapped on the dancing cane (which left me with two minutes of dancing cane music to fill) so I turned dancing cane into a tap dance routine, holding the cane horizontally, like I did when I was eight years old.

The act closed with me doing a dancing handkerchief dressed as Michael Jackson (don't ask, he-he), and at the very end instead of taking the tablecloth off and making the girl appear, I did the dancing handkerchief a little longer than I should have and I walked offstage to two people clapping out of the thousand people and I looked at the guy holding the curtain rope, and I yelled at the guy "close the f- ing curtain!", not knowing this was Fr. Cyprian, now knowing this was the contest chairman who happened to be a priest. That was a great moment in my young catholic life!

From onstage, I heard "hey you! A-hole!" and I turn back around and my girl was under the table, ready to finish the routine! She had found a way to sneak around to her secret hiding spot, with her legged wrapped with a ripped table cloth, and I didn't know she was there ready, waiting, to finish the act. We drove home, I dropped her off at the hospital, I went home and said I'm never going back to the convention, I can't be seen again, but my parents convinced me to go back. So I wrote a new name on my name tag (David Oliver), and on my way back to the convention I drove back and that day I met Harry Blackstone, Norm Nielson, Stan Allen, Mike Caveny, Tina Lenart, and Charlie Reynolds. I got to talk to all these people who didn't know I was that kid in the competition, because I had a different name badge on and was wearing a baseball hat. I ended up making so many new friends and connections that it was both the best and the worst day in my magic life at that point.

Don't bite off more than you can chew. Know your limits. Be overly prepared. I was prepared, but I was not overly prepared. I choose to do a routine I had never done before in public. It was a fresh routine, a cold routine, that had no flight time whatsoever. If I had done a time-tested routine that I was comfortable with, I may have placed in the competition, because I would have known the act inside and out. But here I was with my ego, trying to impress everybody and it didn't work.

Be prepared for anything... don't let the situation control you. You need to control the situation. People that have been students of mine have heard me talk about the MEATcase- Magicians Emergency Accessory Tote*. It's an emergency kit with everything you could need to repair props, costumes, or yourself from band aids, markers, different types of tapes, needle and thread, coat hangers, tweezers, glues, you name it... anything that can go wrong will go wrong. Having a contingency plan for everything is a must. There will always be unexpected obstacles that can't be thrown by. Take it as a challenge and work through it and stay in control.

"Make bold choices and make mistakes. It's all those things that add up to the person you become."
-Angelina Jolie

I first saw **Oz Pearlman** while sitting in Radio City Music Hall watching the finals of America's Got Talent in 2015. Watching him work in one of the biggest venues in the world was, simply put, inspiring. It didn't come as a surprise when he finished third, out of the thousands of acts that auditioned. In addition to AGT, he's appeared on *The TODAY Show, Late Night with Jimmy Fallon,* and *ABC World News*. He has now been dazzling audiences with his unique mind-reading ability for over a decade and has garnered a client list that reads like a who's who of politicians, pro athletes, A-list celebs, and Fortune 500 companies.

The best life lesson for me I learned early on when I had to fend for myself. I had to pay for things at a really, really young age. In my early teenage years, starting when I was about thirteen, all of my disposable income, bills, car, pretty much everything was bought by myself. I didn't really have anyone to rely on. If you have a safety net, you tend to think in the mindset of "hey, whatever! They'll just pay for it, I don't have to do anything". If you don't have a safety net, then you're not falling off that tightrope! You'll be a lot more focused. So I think that knowing nobody was going to do something for me made me much more self-sufficient and able to pull things off that otherwise I would have been much lazier in doing. I think laziness tends to come from options. If you have the option to be lazy, you'll be lazy!

Find your goals. Some people are just hobbyists. If you're a hobbyist and you're having a lot of fun with it and you love learning magic and you love entertaining your friends and your family, then by all means do that! There's no right or wrong set of parameters for anybody. But what if you want to become a semi-professional, or a professional magician? Then that changes the game entirely. I would caution somebody before making the decision to go full time to know exactly what you're getting into. There's nothing wrong with going full time, and I think a great living can be made performing (which is surprising, but true). I know many, many people that do very well, some do extraordinarily well, like more than you can probably make doing virtually any other job, besides being the CEO of a major company. So it is possible that you can rise to a certain level and do a tremendous amount of events and market yourself effectively, but I think that you need to know what you're getting into which is not just performing, but show BUSINESS. You have to know the back end of things, you have to know how to manage well, and have to know how to execute back office things like administrative tasks, people skills, contracts, and calling. You need the same skills you would need to run any other business. You have to be a business person to do well in show business, unless you're fortunate enough to be able to surround yourself by other people who can do that for you. But generally, most people can't do that at the beginning- they can't afford to. So that's why I would caution somebody, but if you're a young magician, have fun! There's no need to rush ahead. When I was a teenager if you would have told me, "hey, you need to do this and this and this," I think I would have been scared off. If you're having fun with it, then that's going to emerge in your performances and in your demeanor.

I used to love reading magic books and learning new tricks and all those things made magic a passion. It wasn't somebody forcing me. It wasn't like when you took violin lessons and you're thinking "ugh I don't want to do this, my parents are making me." As soon as it becomes a chore, you're going to lose a lot of the excitement and passion. So keep that motivation up and keep having fun.

Early on, the most crucial resource to me and my career were books. I think that the lion's share of what I learned was from books. However, when you learn one thing, you think you know what you're doing. But then when you get out there and perform you get real life feedback. The best feedback I ever received was at restaurants. A restaurant is not like when somebody hires you for a show. A restaurant consists of an audience that almost never expects you to be there- they're not expecting you to walk up to their table, and they might not even necessarily want you there. Until you prove to them that they want you there, they have no reason to give you the time of day! You're invading their private space. You don't know how often they go out to eat, so this could be a special night for them, and you're kind of going into their space. Those thousands of nights at restaurants, from the age of fourteen until about four or five years ago, taught me how to work a crowd, how to win people over, and that was the greatest training ever.

Mentors are also really good. If you can seek somebody out, do it. Most people are scared to ask, but if you see someone you admire- say David Blaine- write him an email! He might not write back to you, he might be really busy, but you never know until you reach out. I have a lot of people who are magicians that I spent years writing to, helping, that just reached out to me in a respectful manner and said "hey, how's it going, I like this about you, I'm really happy with what you've done, and I'd like to learn a little bit more" and then they'll ask me a series of really well thought-out questions. I don't like when they just ask "hey, how did you do this trick". I'm not going to reply to that. But for people who obviously want to learn, then most magicians are willing to help! And our business is so complex that it is essential to get all the help we can in order to be prepared for whatever our clients may throw our way.

Catastrophes generally start to occur whenever you let the client take charge of the show and start dictating what you're going to do and how you're going to do it. I had a show where it was customized content. Customized content means I'm doing a show, but I'm incorporating the client's message into it. This particular show was promoting a city. There were city officials there that bought advertisements to let everyone know about their city's attractions. In these type of shows, I usually like to tell the audience two or three bullet points and weave them into my show and not over-do it, but they wanted me to give ten bullet points in an eight or nine minute performance. So it pretty much sounded like I was a bad salesman! It was simply overkill. A couple of days before the event, they also said "hey, it would be a real hoot if we brought up the vice president of the company and we're going to have him appear out of a life size genie lamp, and we're going to have smoke and this woman who works for us is going to have a sexy genie costume and everything!" I'm just sitting there nodding, but in the back of my head I'm thinking that all of this sounds like a disaster. When I get there multiple things happen. They wanted me to use some of the people who work with them to help in the show. It was very hard to do because they don't know what I'm doing and they don't really do what I ask them to do. So, long story short, the smoke machine in the genie lamp onstage doesn't stop, so the stage is completely filled with smoke. You can barely see us, we're coughing up a storm. Next, I have somebody go out and they're supposed to collect slips and let's just say she screwed up in how she collected the slips. It was my fault for not watching her, but I couldn't see anything because of all the smoke. So she gets back onstage (keep in mind that this is in front of about three thousand people), and what should have been a very clean force, did not get forced correctly. So let's just say the volunteer picked the wrong thing. However, I don't know that he's picked the wrong thing because I didn't see it happen. I thought everything was a-okay, but it was one of those situations where if you knew it went wrong you can unwind. Like if someone didn't pick a classic force, you just ask them to pick another one and another one... you can work your way into a solution. But you can't work your way into a solution if you think you've got it right! So I'm planning on doing a production where I produce a big bottle of wine, and then I realize that this guy isn't thinking of a bottle of wine. It was so awkward, and everybody saw me sweating, but I somehow pulled it off. It was a huge disaster in my mind, but to the client, it just looked like I was a little bit all over the place. But I came to a resolution, and the client, if you can believe it, shockingly hired me again for something else. However here I was, onstage, and I couldn't have been more shocked had you walked up and punched me right in the stomach! The air was just gone from my lungs when I realized I got it wrong. I was about to produce the bottle of wine when I realized, and I looked over at the girl who was collecting the slips, and I just realized I was totally screwed because of the smoke. At that point in my career, it was the biggest show I had done in my life.

That day I learned to say no to clients. It's important to know that you're the expert, and although you of course want to make people happy, sometimes they don't know what they're doing and you just need to be gentle and inform them that, based on your experience, you think this won't be the best thing to do and give them another option to consider. You never want to tell someone they are an idiot (even if they are), you just want to guide them in a direction that you "think might work better", even if you know 100% it will be better. I learned that day that I will never let somebody screw up my show because it's all on me at the end. I can't call three thousand people and say "hey, I told them don't do this genie lamp, and don't do this and don't do that." It's YOU who's up there being represented!

"You will only fail to learn if you do not learn from failing."
-Stella Adler

In America the name David Copperfield is synonymous with grand-scale illusions. But these days in Asia, that name is **JC Sum**. He's teleported himself, cars, and spectators across rivers and countries, he's predicted the national lottery, and he's made people vanish from mid-air. When he's not breaking boundaries, he's doing 3500 shows in 34 countries on 4 continents, performing for most of the Fortune 500 companies in Asia, entertaining royalty, being the star of his own magic TV Series, and of course living as a favorite among the public. Having released a bunch of great books himself, he gave me some great tips on releasing the one you're reading right now. He's a terrific guy, and I encourage you to Google him and check out some of the amazing stunts and illusions he's created.

I'll share with you one onstage occurrence, that although I won't call it a disaster, it's a funny incident. I'm performing in the Middle East in Oman. As you may know, it's a Muslim country- very religious. There was royalty at the event and we got a briefing before the show, it's a big illusion show, and they say the girls have to be covered up and not show too much skin as it's disrespectful to the Royal Family, the religion, etc. They didn't want any exposure, so we went out of our way to modify the costumes to cover up even bare shoulders and arms. Everything was fine, there was really no problem of exposure for the girls, and I was doing the show (performing Crystal Metamorphosis- my design for a see-through sub trunk) and it's a very physical illusion, because it's jumping on and off the trick.

Long story short, I split my pants. This was about two-thirds into the show, I was wearing jeans, but it ripped in the back from the butt to all the way down to the calf! This was a really big rip, and obviously the exposure wasn't from the girls, but potentially from my end! But it was in the back and I knew it ripped, so I had to make sure I never turned my back to the audience. In general, in performance, I never turn my back to the audience unless it's deliberate or choreography for an illusion, so it was still alright, but just in some moments when I would normally turn to open a door, I would actually back up to it and move my hand back. So my crew and the people onstage knew that something was wrong, but they didn't really know what. Luckily, I don't think the audience actually knew it! But it definitely threw me off, and I definitely had to think two steps ahead, thinking if there was any point when I had to turn my back! I've always been paranoid about these things so for the longest time I've always wore black underwear under my clothes. So even if something goes wrong- like you don't zip up your fly and you're in black pants, that's where the black art comes in so hopefully you don't flash in a bad way! Since then, I don't really perform in jeans anymore when I'm doing illusions. Now I wear dress pants, with a little flexibility and give so there's a bit of a stretch, but it's not like spandex or lycra. Even leather could be tough because if you sweat, it will stick to you and get all stiff. Especially if you're doing illusions and you have to jump up and down on props, it could be very restrictive. One thing I've always done from early on in my career is always checking my fly before I go onstage. It's never happened to me when my fly is down, but it's something I'm paranoid about!

Part of my work is working on cruise ships, and for cruise ships it's very typical for acts to "fly in" or "fly on"- so you would fly on to do you show for one or two cruises, then you would fly off to another ship or just fly back to land. Fly on acts tend to be stand up acts, so a lot of comedians or stage magicians. With illusionists, we don't typically do fly on acts... normally we are grounded on the ship for a certain amount of time, simply because all our gear is difficult to ship. This is what I've been doing for years. Now a little bit ago I was just joining a ship in Japan. I prepared my equipment a month earlier, but I knew that there were some issues with the logistics company (who is based out of Miami) and they picked up my props quite late, maybe about ten days before I was supposed to join the ship in Japan. That's ample time (it only takes about three days to get shipped out, and maybe another two days for customs). Anyway, I flew from Singapore to Japan to join the ship. It's a long flight, then I joined the ship and normally I would check the schedule to find out when during the week I would perform. Typically I would perform at least one day after I arrive, in order to get settled in and rested, especially if there was jet lag, but on occasion I would have to perform the day I arrive. Typically I would arrive in the late morning/ early afternoon and sometimes they would schedule me to perform that night. Of course no entertainer likes to do that, but that's part of the gig. For the illusion show this is especially very, very tough. Imagine you have to uncase all your illusions, build up all the props, go through tech, mark up the stage, work with the lighting designer, which can take 2-3 hours, work with a new stage crew that aren't a "magic crew", and then do a show. For illusionists this is probably the worst situation- to arrive and know that you have to perform that day.

So I checked in with the production manager and realized that my props never made it to the ship. Well, long story short, the props would not be joining the ship and I had a show that night, and no gear. For a second I thought about cancelling the show, but cancelling the show has it's own problems, because you're already billed to perform that night on the public schedule, if you cancel the ship would have to find a replacement. They could probably look for the on-board resident performers like the singers or dancers, and that means activating people last minute who might either be off for the day, and it just creates a logistical nightmare. So although it's tough, it's better for the performer not to cancel. You also want to put yourself into the position of a commercial performer who is reliable, and that means no matter what the situation is the show must go on.

I thought about for a bit, and I said don't worry, I'll have a show ready. At that point, the show was scheduled to start in 9 hours. So basically I had a few things with me- I always carry a thumb tip, coins, and my camera and gear for projections. I took a cab to the town, went to the department store, and built a show! I shopped around for an hour, grabbed all sorts of stuff, came back, and started having an arts and crafts session in my cabin. After I built the tricks, I practiced and put together all the light and sound cues, went for rehearsals with the crew, and did the show that night! It went perfectly well, no one was the wiser, everyone was happy, and there was a good show! The key to this really was remaining calm and having a strong domain of knowledge in magic. Not just with illusions but with all aspects of magic. I've worked with many shows over my career, from close up shows to parlour shows, and I practice a lot of my close up still today (and I include some of my close up in my illusion show anyway), so I was really pooling all these effects that I've learned over the years to form a show, and then re-editing the music for this impromptu show. There was still production value- with lighting cues- but it wasn't an illusion show as I would have done if I had my gear.

In my opinion, illusions are an evolution of you being a magician. You need to start off with your general conjuring skills before you become an illusionist, because being an illusionist requires being more involved than being just a regular magician. You do need to have a very good foundation of a regular magician- close up, sleight of hand, misdirection, stage management, audience management, you need to get all of this down pat and continue to improve it and learn as you get into illusions. It doesn't mean that just because I'm an illusionist I can forgo my basic conjuring skills and just rely on my assistants, dancers, crew, smoke and lights, etc. A show is still very much based on the performer. The magic comes from the performer, not the props. If you ever transfer the responsibility to the illusion props or the stage equipment to create the show, that's when I think the show suffers. The one piece of advice I would offer the aspiring illusionist is to continually hone your general magic skills.

The best lesson I was ever taught was one I read about. There's this book by Mark Walker- The Master Illusionist- published in 1983. It's a collection of interviews with master illusionists of that time, and some that are still masters today- Siegfried and Roy, David Copperfield, Mr. Electric, Jonathan Pendragon, etc. It wasn't just confined to stage magicians, but close up magicians too. More or less the same questions were asked to all of these different masters and they gave opinions of things and one question asked was about the importance of being different. There were two vastly opposing views. Jonathan Pendragon viewed that being different was not that important... what is more important is to be excellent. If you have an excellent craft, excellent performance, than that is the most important, it's all that's needed to rise to the top. If you think about the Pendragons, they were doing the classics and while he did invent a lot of illusion techniques and designs of props, the emphasis was definitely on peak performance and being good.

Now on the other hand, Mr. Electric (Marvyn Roy) thought that you don't have to be great (you can't be bad, though), but what's more important is to be different. He called it the Meatball act- rather than do a dove act or a silk act, he would rather you do a meatball act where you make meatballs appear and disappear, because at least then you would be different. And by being different, you would stand out. These are two really opposing views, and personally I feel that being different is very important, but I take more of an in between approach.

Being great to me is a given. As illusionists and magicians, we have to be great. When laymen watch a juggler or listen to a singer, they can tell if they are good. If the juggler drops things people can tell he isn't good. If a singer cracks, people can tell she isn't good. For a magician, by virtue of our art, everything should go right. When everything goes right and the audience has no idea what happened, they really don't know how good we are. It's only other magicians who can appreciate sophisticated technique, or methods, or designs. But as far when laymen are concerned, they can't judge how good a magician is as long as they are being fooled. If you vanish something by sleeving it, topiting it, or tossing it behind black art, the audience won't know. That's why I think being good has its limits. But a lay audience member can recognize a magician being different. "Oh I've never seen it before! "That approach seems fresh!" "This character seems new!" So this really stuck with me and being different is something that I've kept in whatever I do... I try to make sure there is some difference. I can't say I am the most original guy on the block in terms of being pure creative- meaning creating stuff that has never been seen or done before. But I'm quite good at innovating- taking something old and making it fresh, making it different, or commercially appealing. That in and of itself is a difference. There are many ways to be different, but it's important to be different and to stand out. For many commercial performers, the only difference in the lay people's eye is the price. That's when clients will start to bargain with you... If you're a commodity and the same as the next guy, then they'll base their decision on purely price. However if you perform in a different way, or do a different illusion, then you can justify your price by saying that nobody else does what I do. And that was what Mr. Electric meant when he discussed his meatball act- if no one else does it, then comparing it to other magicians is like comparing apples and oranges. One of my business and marketing concepts, which is the cornerstone of my business, is positioning. A concept by Elvis. Positioning is about positioning yourself in the minds of the market and the consumers. So if you think of hamburgers, you think of McDonalds. Pizza, you might think of Pizza Hut. So the idea is that you own a position in the minds of an audience member. The only way to do that is to have some difference between you and your competition.

"All men make mistakes, but only wise men learn from their mistakes."
-Winston Churchill

Boris Wild is one of the most renowned French magicians in the world. He is a performer, author, creator, and lecturer. His performances have drawn thousands of spectators from all over the world: London, New York, Las Vegas, Monte Carlo, Sydney, and Tokyo. His creativity and original approach to magic allows him to perform for the biggest companies in the most prestigious places in the world, including The Magic Castle in Hollywood where he has performed hundreds of shows. He's been the guest of honor at the coveted FFFF convention, he's won awards at FISM, and has a line of best-selling books, effects, and videos. Although Boris is the only contributor who I did not get to interview directly due to his incredibly busy travel and performance schedule, he was kind enough to email me the segment that you are about to read. Enjoy!

I was doing a lecture tour in the United States in 2003 so I rented a car to go from one city to another. My schedule was quite tight with a lecture everyday for about two weeks, I had no cell phone and there was no navigation system in the car. I left Chicago in the morning knowing I had to drive to Louisville, KY for a lecture in evening. The person who was arranging the lectures for me told me it would be about a 4-5 hours drive. And I believed him! I left my hotel in Chicago at 10am and started to drive. Hour after hour, I realized the trip would be much longer than expected but I drove carefully on Interstate 70 at 70 mph, knowing US cops do not joke with speed.

I was driving around Indianapolis when I looked in my mirror and saw a police car following me with all the lights flashing. I did not know what was happening but I pulled over to the side of the road. The policeman came to my car and asked for my driver's license. I handed him my French driver's license and he looked at it like I was giving him something from another planet. While he was looking at my license with a puzzled face, I asked him why he asked me to pull over. He told me the speed limit was 50 mph and I was driving at 70 mph. I told him I saw signs saying "70" but they were in fact "Interstate 70" signs as the speed limit was 50 mph for a couple of miles around Indianapolis! I He admitted it was a great place for speed trap and that is why he was always there! I made him notice I was driving on the right lane of a four-lane road, I did not pass anybody but a lot of cars passed me! He told me "Maybe, but you are the one I saw". Then after hearing my accent, he asked me where I was from. You have to remember it was a time when France and the USA were not the best friends in the world because of the war in Iraq. So I answered: "From Europe...". He asked me: "Where in Europe?". I said: "The middle of Europe...... France.". And I thought: "Okay, I'm dead now!". Then he said: "Oh you are from France! My wife and I went to Paris a few years ago and we had a wonderful time. Where are you going like this?". I told him I was on my way to Louisville and he said I still had a few more hours driving. He went to his car and made me wait in mine for at least 15 minutes. It looked like to me it was 3 hours!

Then he came back with a piece of paper and said: "This is not a ticket, it is just a warning. Pin it on your wall at home to show your friends you have been arrested by the police in the US but be careful, you are now filed in Indiana so do not drive over the speed limit again or it will get much worse for you". I was so relieved. I thanked him and took the road again to Louisville. But all of this delayed me so much. I drove carefully for a couple of hours until I realized I had about one more hour driving to get to the lecture. It was almost 5:45pm and the lecture was at 7pm. I could still be on time but without eating or setting up everything the way I usually do. I decided to make a stop and find a phone booth to call the person in charge of the lecture in Louisville and tell him he should not worry as I was on my way. I did it and he told me: "Well, you'd better be quick because the lecture is in 15 minutes and everybody is already there!". I said: "What???

I thought the lecture was at 7pm, not 6pm". And he told me: "Yes, the lecture is at 7pm and it is 6:45pm right now!" I did not know there was a one-hour time difference between Chicago and Louisville!! Nobody told me that! I drove so much that I changed time zones! Quite unusual for a European guy who is not used to changing the hour of his watch when he takes his car to drive several hours.

I quickly hung up, rushed to the car and told myself: "Now Boris, you have two possibilities: Option #1: After what happened to you, you drive safely and you are VERY late and it is not right for the people waiting for you. Plus you hate being late. Or Option #2: You drive fast, you arrive with a "reasonable" delay but you take the risk to be caught by the cops again and in that case, you finish your evening in a cell!!"

So which option do you think I picked? Yes, number 2! I drove really fast until the place of the lecture and, thank God, there was no cop on the road. When I arrived, I rushed to the restrooms, I undressed there and changed my clothes pretty much in the middle of everybody. I quickly set up all my props and the lecture started just before 7:30pm. I came in front of everybody, out of breath, and said: "Sorry for the slight delay but here I am and enjoy the next two hours of magic!" I was nervously exhausted but the lecture went very well and it was very successful.

I will never forget that day and I learned one important lesson: always check the time differences when you travel even if you do not fly!

For nearly a decade, **Rob Zabrecky's** ambitiously unique and offbeat performances at the Magic Castle, where he is a prime attraction, have led him to become recognized as one of the club's top acts. He has received multiple award nominations by the Academy of Magical Arts. As a magical humorist, he creates a dryly abstracted, austere universe that pushes magic to its very edges and often explores bizarre and contemplative human behavior. MAGIC Magazine hailed, "Zabrecky's magic could easily be the plot line of a Stephen King novel, if Steven King wrote comedy." His absurdist and deadpan humor have delighted audiences from Tokyo to New York City. I first met Rob in February of 2017 and he was kind enough to give me some time and help me with an act I upon which I was working on. Of course, his critiques were spot on and it showed me that not only is he a great magician, but a great guy as well.

A couple of years ago I was hired to perform at an airport. It was an after dinner thing for an annual party. Usually they have different entertainment and this year the guy who was booking it wanted me to come and do magic. I was hired to do a 45 minute show. I get to this airplane hangar and there's fifty pilots all who had finished dinner and were drinking. The hangar is this massive room, and if something should go wrong, this is the place because it's so big that people can't hear a word you're saying. There are sounds going off everywhere, it's bouncing off the walls. There's aviation equipment everywhere so you're kind of dodging planes to talk to people. So here I am, all set up, when I see a handful of young ladies, scantily dressed, walk in and head into a back room. I ask what's going on in there and the guy tells me that usually they have some strippers come in to dance for these men and that's the entertainment, but tonight we're going to give them a magic show. I knew right then that I'm a goner.

These guys all know that I'm the guy that's in between them and the lap dances and whatever else is going to go on in this situation. I walk onstage and it's weird to think that you'd be booed by a bunch of pilots and they didn't verbally boo me but by their eyes and their mannerisms and by turning their backs to me, it was clear they wanted no part in this. Now, in my show I need a dozen spectators- 'think of a card', 'think of a color', and what not. But these men were literally rejecting me and shaking their heads non-verbally asking when would this be done so the ladies could come out. So my

45 minute show turned into a 15 minute show and as I finished my last trick which is to music, there was no applause. Zero applause. As in nothing. All fifty guys were looking at me thinking *just get off the stage*. And lo and behold, as I scurry off stage and in walk these girls ready to party- the room lit up! It was like night and day. It was pretty depressing. As a magician you're thrust into these weird parties and events and these are all things that can hurt your ego and feelings. It's important to know and understand when it's the right time to walk away and say "I'm not doing this".

This plays into my biggest mistake- a mistake that I've made many times in my professional career- the mistake of not saying "no". In the beginning and really up until a few years ago, I would take jobs I wasn't qualified to do and then realizing when I got to the job "I really should not be doing this" whether it be a walk-around thing or just something I was the wrong choice for. These types of mistakes end up with feelings of depression and 'what am I doing with my life?'. But then I remember that I chose this. I made this happen. Everyone has felt this way, and for me time is the best remedy. Time allows me to reflect on those moments and think 'where did I go wrong?' and 'how can I not make this mistake again?' And then make smart decisions from there and try to do things that are more well suited to what I do and how I want to be seen, perceived, and to go along with what kind of art I want to put into the world. As an early magician, I look back and think 'why on earth did I do that event?' and I think to myself 'I'll never do that again', but then a week later the phone rings and I would do the same thing, because I'm a human and humans are flawed and think we can do things that we can't. So I think over a long period of time, I've realized what my strengths and weaknesses are- for example, someone just reached out to me and asked if I could do sleight of hand in a film. My instinct is 'yea, I can backpalm, do split fans, I can probably do this' but I spent some time thinking about this and realized I'm not right for this job. It's for a cardistry person who is at a higher level than me and spends eight hours a day on this exact thing and it's not for some jerk who just wants to make $500. Know your weaknesses, know what you can do, but most importantly know what you can't do. This involves a sense of humility.

You always have to find little things to be humbled by, because otherwise you can start taking things for granted. It's something that you have to work into your core values- like the idea of being grateful and knowing that no matter how much you are putting into the art pool, there's a lot more that can be taken away. It's a daily thing that I think we all need to bring into our lives to become better magicians as well as better people.

Magic is an art form and one can really express themselves as a magician as they could in life if they were an actor, painter, dancer, or a songwriter. For me, getting into magic later I didn't realize that because the role-models and examples didn't inform me of that. However, when I got into music there were so many colorful musicians and different kinds of music I was attracted to- it was this open playing field. Yet I didn't really see the art of magic until I dove in at the Magic Castle, and that's when I really started seeing that it's an art form, and at times a greatly neglected one. 80% of practitioners are buying a trick from the magic store and following the instruction or learning the youtube routine and practicing it exactly. This results in a poor carbon copy with no unique point of view. Then you've got 500 guys doing an egg bag the same way with the same lines and it's not funny, it's not interesting, and it's certainly not entertaining.

Take more emotional risks. So much of our time and our lives are spent getting up in the morning, getting ready, going to the bank, showering, putting food in our bodies, and all those things. By the time we step into the spotlight- onstage or in a walk around performance- we need to be special. We need to be extraordinary beings. We need to be able to take people away from their problems and give them a world to go into. However we can't do that if we're doing the stock lines that come with the trick. We've got to put ourselves out there and the emotional risks come from really writing ourselves in our material and exposing ourselves. It's scary and can be dangerous emotionally, and that's why a lot of people don't do this. But the ones that do make all the difference and that's why artists like Ricky Jay, Penn and Teller, Mac King, and Derek DelGaudio have really stretched the boundaries.

For me to stretch my boundaries, The Magic Castle has been such a great resource. I have this playground to find a spot to do something I'm working on, to be inspired, to talk to other magicians, and to really be a part of this community. Finding a magic community and a theater community (because I think they're equally as important) to immerse yourself in is incredibly important because the aforementioned elements are just what one needs to be pushed in the right direction.

Learn from your mistakes and move on. Some of us continue to blow it in the same ways, and we can all be in better places if we cut our losses and move forward.

Ben Zabin has been an entertainer since the tender age of 4. Starting off his career by taking the magic competition circuit by storm, Ben became the proud holder of over a dozen international awards and honors at an early age. His unique brand of magic has been seen on stages from off-Broadway in New York City, to the famous Rio Hotel and Casino in Las Vegas, and everywhere in between. In addition to performing over 60 shows a year across the country, he is the producer of his own magic kit product line, and is the go-to magic consultant for the Huffington Post. In 2016, he was named one of the "Top 10 Teens to Watch" by Moffly Media. When he's not onstage, he enjoys producing live events and working on projects such as this book. He also enjoys writing bios in the third person. Keep up with Ben by following him on social media: @BenZabinMagic and learn more by visiting www.BenZabin.com

Made in the USA
Columbia, SC
25 June 2018